Going Over East

Other books by Linda Hasselstrom

Caught by One Wing
Roadkill
Windbreak
Land Circle: Writings Collected from the Land

Books edited by Linda Hasselstrom

James Clyman: Journal of a Mountain Man
Next-Year Country: One Woman's View

Going Over East
Reflections of a Woman Rancher

Linda Hasselstrom

FULCRUM PUBLISHING
Golden, Colorado

Copyright © 1987 Linda M. Hasselstrom

Book Design by Chris Bierwirth
Cover Design and Illustration by Paulette Livers Lambert

First Fulcrum trade paperback edition published March 1993.

Library of Congress Cataloging-in-Publication Data

Hasselstrom, Linda M.
Going Over East.
1. Hasselstrom, Linda M.—Biography.
2. Authors, American—20th century—Biography.
3. Ranchers—South Dakota—Biography.
4. Ranch life—South Dakota.
I. Title.
PS3558.A7257Z465   1987   818'.5409   [B]   87-12071
ISBN   1-55591-018-1
ISBN   1-55591-141-2 (pbk.)

Printed in the United States of America

0   9   8   7   6   5   4   3   2   1

Fulcrum Publishing
350 Indiana Street, Suite 350
Golden, Colorado 80401-5093

Acknowledgments

A portion of "The Home Place" first appeared in slightly different form as "A shot of used grass" in *High Country News*, Vol. 17, No. 24.

A portion of "Shade for the Prancing Horse" appeared as "Beauty" in *Horizons: The South Dakota Writers' Anthology* (Hermosa, S.D.: Lame Johnny Press, 1983).

CONTENTS

Introduction

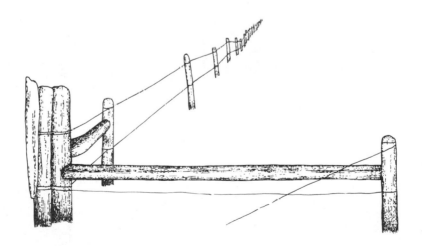

I was nine years old. I don't remember my birthday that year, but a month later, on August 14, I was adopted by my mother Mildred's new husband. A photograph shows me on adoption day in a ruffled plaid dress in front of the old brick courthouse, clutching a little white purse with white shoes perfectly aligned. I'm smiling stiffly. Adoption was a new experience.

After the ceremony my legal father, John, bought me a gold ring I still have, and we all had ice cream. I didn't realize that by becoming the daughter of a rancher I had changed the direction of my life forever. I didn't realize I had pledged my soul to a ranch, to acres of tawny grass and dry creeks that would absorb my blood and sweat, as they had my father's, and still look parched. I was still dreaming of prancing black stallions; now my dreams are full of waddling cows.

A couple of months after my name changed, my father announced that we were "going over east" to get the cows out of summer pasture. The day was cold and blustery. He and my mother and I climbed into the green 1949 Chevrolet truck (we still have it) and headed out over the brown plains. He would stop at a gate, get out, open it, get back in the truck, drive through the gate, get out, close the gate and get back in. I hadn't yet learned that opening gates was to be one of my jobs. Off in the distance were the knife-sharp ridges of the Badlands, looking blue and icy.

It seemed to me we drove for hours, and the Badlands slowly got closer until we slipped down into a small valley, still green, with the clouds low and gray

3

above us. Then my mother shifted the pickup into super low and led the cattle while my father and I walked behind them.

Before long, snow began to fall heavily, muffling all sound and cutting off my view at the tops of the low hills nearby. I could hear nothing but the moaning wind, see nothing but a few brown and white cows, who looked at me, snorted, then turned and ran ahead. Suddenly I felt very small, alone and terrified—until, dimly, I saw the tall, slightly bent figure of my father, almost lost in the blowing snow. He was striding along, looking sure of where he was and where he was going. That may have been the moment when I really began to know him.

Now, thirty-five years later, that stooped figure still dominates the ranch and "going over east." I've realized since what I only suspected that day: that someone who pays attention to the messages the natural world sends can bring cattle home the day *before* a blizzard nine times out of ten. It's a matter of instinct, experience, self-reliance. I had no landmarks in the blizzard; similarly, I've found few rules in the business of ranching. You learn by doing it.

The Hasselstrom family has ranched on the South Dakota prairie since the late 1800s, when my grandfather Charles came here from Sweden, after repaying the price of his passage by working on the farm of relatives in Iowa. A covey of Swedes and Norwegians crossed the plains and homesteaded close together in what must have seemed a vast emptiness. Charles

Introduction

Hasselstrom married Ida Sanders Callahan, who had come with her family from Missouri to western South Dakota, married, been widowed, and was homesteading with her children. Together, they produced five more offspring, including my stepfather—referred to always as my father. My uncle Harold, who ranches a few miles northwest of us, is my father's oldest brother.

My mother's family also came west from Missouri, and settled in the southern Black Hills. Schooling and marriage took her away from the area, but divorce brought her back with a daughter. Three of her brothers live in the region, and one, George, ranches about sixty miles southwest of us.

The ranch that is the site of this series of essays is located in the arid grasslands of western South Dakota near the Black Hills, an area especially well-suited to livestock grazing, and once the range of the buffalo. Similar temperate grasslands exist in only a few other areas of the world: the Uruguayan Pampas, the Pontian Steppe in Russia and Western Europe, a narrow strip in northwestern Africa, the eastern grasslands and savannas of Australia. Early explorers called this area the "Great American Desert" before its fertility was recognized and homesteaders appeared on every horizon.

Today the cycle of public opinion appears to have shifted again, and more populous areas seem to regard the plains as an "empty quarter," fit only for the disposal of garbage, as if it were the country's back alley. Within the past five years, we've entertained proposals for the placement here of: uranium mines and mills, a national hazardous waste disposal site, a national radioactive waste disposal site, a processing and disposal site for sewage ash, several strip mining and heap leach processing operations, a superconducting supercollider, a site for incineration and/or landfilling of PCBs (polychlorinated biphenyls), a sulfide mine, and several sites for the building, testing and disposal of ammunition and other explosive devices. Low population, a crippled agricultural industry, a body of potential employees who used to be farmers, and a lack of factory industry apparently make the area a target for promoters of such plans. A number of hazardous substances have been spilled, and local and state agencies have demonstrated alarming inabilities and ignorance in cleanup. As if that weren't enough, a bill to give a considerable amount of federal forest and grassland back to the Lakota (Sioux) Indians is being seriously debated in Congress.

Since South Dakota's early settlement involved a gold rush (remember Deadwood? Wild Bill Hickok? Calamity Jane?), mining and related industries are still more encouraged than regulated by state law, making it an ideal site for the kind of industries more politically powerful states don't want near population centers. South Dakota has become the Polish joke of states, a symbol of remoteness and isolation, the home of the original bumpkin—even if it did produce Tom Brokaw. Even residents of Garrison Keillor's Lake Woebegon make jokes about South Dakota. A few years ago, the mayor of a small city near our ranch appeared in *Life* magazine holding a piece of radioactive yellowcake in his teeth, to demonstrate his lack of fear and his determination that his town would host a uranium mine, mill and tailings dump. Reporters descended from all over the country, snickering about the town in a state so backward it *wanted* what other states were clamoring to avoid.

If South Dakota had the country's highest mountains, the most beautiful beaches or some strange species of animal, we would get more respect; but all we have is clean air, grass, Mount Rushmore and some pretty good skiing. (A mining company is negotiating to buy the best ski area in the state; they promise not to mine the slopes.)

When I went to graduate school in Missouri, the pre-Ph.D. wits in the English department affected to believe that the earth was flat and ended ten miles north of St. Louis. Beyond that, they insisted, was only a dark, rolling, poisonous cloud, populated by savage cannibals and from which loud noises issued only in election years. I entertained at cocktail parties with tales of a childhood spent with a rifle in each hand for fighting off grizzly bears, Indians and rustlers. Unfortunately, that view of the plains no longer prevails.

Many of the proposals for what is termed "bringing money and jobs into the state" center on the arid western half, while most people who might call themselves "environmentalists" live in the more metropolitan eastern half. Putting together coalitions of individuals dedicated to sensible but environmentally sane development has proven to be complex; ranchers won't talk to members of the Sierra Club, and intellectuals sometimes seem to believe that ranchers live only to slaughter prairie dogs and overgraze public land. As a rancher concerned with conserving the state's pure air as well as its western independence, I have learned it is no longer possible to live in splendid isolation and think only of cows, but the next step is sometimes confusing.

We—my father and mother, my husband and I— run a cow-calf operation, one of the most labor-intensive of ranching businesses. Our way of life, as operators of a one-family ranch, is no longer common, for reasons that include the immense labor and the long hours required for precarious profits.

When we head over east I become, more than at any other time, a composite of a hundred years of history here; the spirits of earlier dwellers in the land seem to follow my pickup like dust. Things I remember from my own past mingle with things my father has told me about his youth, and his father's. A history of this piece of land would require some mingling of the dry official records with the varied and fallible memories of those who have lived and ranched or farmed here. No single truth is possible.

The land exists outside of people's memories. Yet without the men and women who devoted their lives to this land, it wouldn't be the same; they have added a dimension to it by their labor, just as their bodies have added fertility to the poor soil of the little graveyard in Hermosa. My contribution is still being tallied, but when it is finished I will be glad to be, finally, completely absorbed in the land.

Because our way of life may be vanishing beneath the mechanisms of a seemingly more efficient method of raising cattle—corporate ranching—young people are taking stock of their positions. In a modern corporation, responsibility is difficult to assign. Nobody wants to say "the buck stops here." More likely, you'll get a shrug and the all-purpose line, "I just work here." Everyone knows someone who inherited a ranch worth millions of dollars and managed to lose it in a year or two by following that dictum, but successful ranchers don't shrug off responsibility. Running a ranch isn't a nine-to-five job, and you don't leave the work at the office on weekends.

My father's ability to make a living on this ranch is based on his way of doing things. He is careful with a dollar; he learned young the virtue of wearing out a piece of machinery, fixing it himself, making do. He has often repeated to me his main rule of ranching: "Never spend any money." Putting this philosophy into action means that a rancher's family seldom takes a vacation. When they do travel they often stay with relatives. Cattle grazing in the pastures of a man who practices this philosophy won't be as fat as those on the color covers of the farm journals, and when he rounds them up, he'll do it quietly, without much noise—no galloping horses and no whips. He knows his real crop is grass, so he doesn't abuse it, whether it's on his own land or land leased from the government. His "new" four-wheel-drive pickup is probably eight years old, and called that to distinguish it from his "old" 1949 pickup and the secondhand 1963 one he uses mostly for fencing.

I believe in my father's penny-pinching philosophy; I have seen it work. The question is, will it continue to work for me? When my father sent me to college I studied literature instead of tractor mechanics. I've learned a lot about repairing our old equipment, but not everything I need to know, and the community fix-it man is gone now. Production costs rise every year, while worldwide beef production drops, and ranchers often get less money for the beef they produce—even though the price to the consumer has risen. Meanwhile, consumers are nervous about red meat and the things added to it.

I grew up here. The work schedule on the ranch enables me to find time to write, so I'm willing to accept 365 days of hard work a year and a standard of living that does not allow for luxuries many families now take for granted. But can I expect my husband, whose health is a problem, to make the same choice? How long can we keep up the labor as our bodies grow older?

Today I am going over east with my husband, George, and his son, Michael, who stays with us in July and August. As we drive, I try to explain to them something of what this dry, hot land has come to mean to me. My narration is divided into segments according to the gates we pass through en route to our summer pasture.

The Home Place

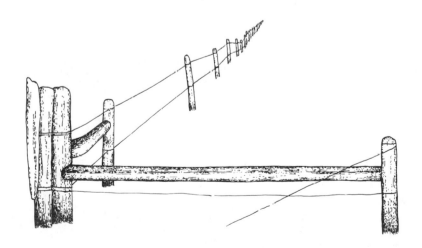

Going over east to our summer pasture on a July day when the temperature at 8:00 A.M. is already a hundred degrees requires preparation. We check the gas, water and oil in the truck, fill extra jugs for drinking and for a hot radiator. I pack a lunch, since we never know exactly how long a trip over east will take. We drive about six miles to the gate where our land begins, and then three miles across to the other end. Depending on the job to be done, the trip has taken as little as three hours and as many as ten.

George and Mike load fencing equipment, tools, posts and shovels. When fire danger is high, we take gunnysacks and a cream can full of water. George adds a bridle, saddle, spurs, in case we need to move cattle; the horse is already pastured over east.

The truck contains various wrenches, extra spark plugs, screwdrivers, a couple of snakebite kits. I added first-aid supplies to the trucks when my father whacked his leg with a shovel and arrived home with his shoe squishy with blood. We also have hats, leather gloves for fencing, suntan lotion for those of us who burn and peel, binoculars that save miles of driving, and George's pistol.

When we've collected most of this stuff we think we're ready for anything, forgetting that Mother Nature has a talent for nasty surprises.

As soon as we leave the shelter of the trees around the house, a wall of heat breaks over the pickup. No rain has fallen for over a month, since a hail that badly damaged my garden. The official average rainfall for our area is slightly over sixteen inches. This is one of the few statistics I know, and I don't believe it. According to my father's careful records, our rainfall amounts in the past four years are as follows: 6.45 inches; 6.15 inches; 17.65 inches; 8.12 inches. That's an average of 9.59 inches, reminding me that believing anything without checking for yourself is risky business.

Since we have a good well, the ranch buildings and our carefully nurtured rows of trees have become a cool, green oasis in the prairie, attracting birds, rabbits, antelope, deer and snakes. Few trees grow naturally in western South Dakota, except along intermittent creeks. Every evening in summer, we watch my father carry bucket after bucket of water to the young trees. A little grove of pines is crowded south of the house. He knows they're too close together; he expected more of them to die, and now he's reluctant to cut any down.

In front of the house, to the west, my mother wanted a real city lawn. My father had to haul in dirt from a creek bottom in order to get it established. Now they spend hours watering, mowing and raking it. On the other sides, the native and introduced grasses—buffalo grass, brome, alfalfa, crested wheat—grow knee high without water. We mow and rake this grass with the tractor, and feed it to the horses.

Still farther west, only a half-mile from the highway, my husband and I built a new home a few years ago. Since neither of us is a carpenter, we were lucky to get the help of friends who are, but we drew the plans and did much of the actual building ourselves, from pouring concrete to putting up walls, shingling the roof and laying up the chimney blocks. A thousand times during the construction process I wished I had studied house-building instead of American literature—but I learned to derive immense satisfaction from the hard physical exertion and working with my hands.

The process of creating a setting for the house—with a windbreak row of cedar trees and buffaloberry and plum bushes—is a slow one, and also largely dependent on hand labor, since the slope of the rock-strewn hill prevents use of a tractor. Our topsoil is a dark gray band no more than four inches thick, beneath which the soil becomes light gray and laced with limestone. Because we have refused to plant a lawn or sculpt the area around our house into an imitation of a city yard, it remains nearly wild. Technically, we're in a mixed-grass prairie region, though many of our plants are characteristic of shortgrass areas, with a maximum grass height of around sixteen inches. The basic grass, the supporter of most of the grazing animals, is the five-inch buffalo grass, short but powerful.

The skunk who dens on the west side of our hillside has learned to avoid digging in the compost pile until the dog is inside. Hawks drift past the windows hunting mice, and occasionally perch on the porch railings to rest. The rabbit that lived in the woodpile for three years is gone, killed by a barn cat. We'll all miss her. I put lettuce scraps by her den in winter, and the dog spent deliriously happy hours trying—without a hope—to catch her. On winter nights, as she hopped around on the snowdrifts, the cat would sit on the windowsill and growl softly, causing us to have strange dreams or to wake and kneel at the window watching the night. But the barn cat was following his nature, and we try to let the wild animals around us live out their natural cycles, whatever they are.

East of the ranch buildings, as we drive out of the tree belt, lie the alfalfa fields—the source, with a place we own near Hermosa, of the hay for our cattle. Here in the bottom of a broad gully, topsoil is richer and darker, and alfalfa roots may reach down until they encounter water—some say from four to ten feet or more. We've cut one crop of alfalfa this summer, and that will be the last unless we get rain soon. The stacks stand huge, golden green; around their bases the alfalfa is sparse, mixed with native grasses. Even the green plants are so dry they crackle.

Hay isn't something we can count on here. The creek place is one of the best pieces of hay land in the area. In 1915 my family put up a thousand tons of hay there, but the next year we harvested only 260 tons. Without the second crop, we have to buy hay or sell cows before winter. Sometimes, instead of cutting a second crop of hay, we harvest alfalfa seed to sell or plant.

One of my first flashes of understanding the complexity of ranching came on a walk through the fields east of the house with my father as he tried to decide whether to mow the fields or leave them for seed. It was August, and had been ninety-nine degrees for days. We'd had no rain since my twelfth birthday in mid-

July, when lightning from a terrible hail- and windstorm had killed my horse.

"Let's walk through it a little and look at what we've got, Daughter." I was always half running and jumping to keep up with his strides.

"Hoppers stripped a lot of it the last few days." I hadn't noticed, but they spun away ahead of us in dozens, wings snapping and glinting in the sun, jaws working with brown juice.

"This is too green yet, just setting on. If we left it, it might freeze before it got podded." He bent double and wrenched off a bunch of stems, crushed them in his palms and poured the fragments from hand to hand. The chaff blew away, leaving broken spiral pods coiled around tiny yellow and brown seeds.

"See, alfalfa's yellow when it's ripe, solid and shiny." He poked at it with a dusty finger, then put some in his mouth, looking into the sun as he tasted it. Shadows striding ahead, we crossed the trail and passed the barely flowing well.

"And, you know, combining's seven dollars an hour now. And they dock you for the weeds when you sell the seed. Last time it cost almost a third of what I made for the combine." The heat seemed to vibrate with the sound of the dry grass whipping against our legs.

"Have to figure on it freezing the first of September, for all practical purposes." He stopped and was rubbing his chin, looking across the fields. "This is just podding on; it'll never be ripe by frost. There's an awful lot of good chewing for the cattle here, though, if I'd just mow it and stack it—even if it is pretty dry. Could wean the calves and turn them in here for a month this fall, let them eat around the stacks."

Up the slope and past an abandoned root cellar we went. "Not much doubt about this; nothing here but weeds. That low spot north of the trees is good, though. He could combine that in half a day if he wasn't busy."

Barn swallows hung above us, hovering, to swing away after insects.

"And then, Daughter, on top of everything else, it's a hell of a fire trap for a man's place when it gets dry like it's been this year. One spark and the whole thing would go."

Any choice in this country is a balancing of the odds, and then taking a gamble anyway. No matter what you decide, the land or weather may have other plans.

We were back in the shade of the trees near the house, leaning on the truck. "God, what we'd have given for a shade tree like this over at the home place. We had one big tree over there, by the well. Did everything under it for years—blacksmithing, fixing harness. We froze ice cream and ate it sitting on the well curb. I suppose Pa packed water to it by the bucketful for years, like I've done with these, only there wasn't ever enough water." He shook his head. "Just when it got to be a big nice tree, the roots broke into the well, and we had to cut it down and pull out the stump to keep from having all the water spoiled. Dad told us boys one morning at breakfast about it, and then went to town. We cut it down and jerked it out with the team before he got back. Don't think he ever mentioned it again."

He got the thermos out of the truck and poured himself half a cup of coffee. I never could understand how he could drink hot coffee when it was ninety degrees in the shade; when I asked, he said it made him cooler. He's right. I always take coffee now when we go over east.

"Well, Daughter," he said, "I guess I'll mow part of it, and leave that low spot by the trees until the combiner can look it over and tell me what he thinks. We can always cut it later if it doesn't freeze or get too dry. But we just might get a little seed this year."

The resources of the ranch are stretched with four people living here, even though my husband and I both have small sources of outside income. We calculate each purchase before we make it. Even buying machinery to make our haying more efficient and less physically demanding might overbalance our delicate economic structure.

As if to remind us of the precariousness of our existence, a two-room homestead cabin sags and sways just northwest of the home place. Pigeons perch on the tilting brick chimney, and the doorway leans toward the north. The next time we get a spring storm that dumps a foot of wet snow on the roof, the structure will probably fold up like a house of cards.

Behind it, sinking into the grass, is an old horse-drawn hay stacker. Generally, salvage is a fine art in ranch country. Fence posts that were six feet tall when they were set thirty years ago, but have rotted at the bottom, are dug out, turned over, and set in a stretch of fence where height isn't as important. Plank corral gates are heavy, and miserable to shut when the mud is deep in spring; as we can afford it, we're replacing them with gates made of metal. But the old plank gate is fitted into the corral fence somewhere, and wired into place. No matter how outmoded something may be, it is used, re-used, and altered for another use until it falls apart.

But no one made use of the oak tines of the old stacker. When tractors invaded the country, the old horse-drawn implements were parked and left to molder in their own time. I suppose a few old men looked back, cursing the popping motor of the tractor and longing for their team of horses, but most moved into the modern age with confidence in the power of invention to make their work easier. The horse harnesses hang in the barn loft, dusty and cracking with neglect. Anyone who uses horses now is either rich enough to indulge in them as a pastime, a member of a religious sect like the Amish, or "one of them hippies." Yet when we have the annual spring blizzard that dumps three feet of wet snow on top of two feet of mud, immobilizing the tractors, someone invariably remarks that horses could get through it.

About ten years ago an old man drove into the yard and asked permission to look at the homestead cabin. "It belonged to my folks," he explained. We opened the gates for him, and asked for more details. He reminisced; a hundred people came to their farewell party, and somehow crowded into a space less than thirty feet square. A mile to the east, easily visible from this little knoll, stand the remains of another cabin, with stone walls on the first floor and a frame second floor. It, too, is heading for the ground now. A few years ago, when I used to play house in it, or tie my horse outside and take shelter from a sudden rainstorm, it still held the hand-carved mantel and beautifully crafted cupboards made by its owner. But it's too close to a public road; vandals destroyed what they couldn't take with them.

The deep-blue Vicks bottles that line the windows of my study, flashing blue light like prisms, all came from the dump behind the nearer homestead. Some friends have, with permission, taken boards for rustic picture frames from a pile of lumber outside. When the building drops into the grass and begins decaying more rapidly, little will be left to remind the eye that a family chose this spot as their home. I suppose the old man is dead now; when we're gone, no one will remember him, and a few years after that, few will remember us.

But that's looking too far ahead. Our immediate concerns are closer. A rancher heading out to look at his cows never looks straight ahead at the trail. I'm unconsciously looking south, checking the cattle in the pasture we're passing. They're gathered around the water hole, which may mean something's wrong. The water here trickles from the top of the well, unusual in this dry country and technically illegal. But the water has encouraged willows to grow in the gully, and bands of antelope and deer, flocks of grouse, killdeer, coyotes and other wildlife seem to prefer to drink here, where they can hide.

The cows have tramped the hose from the well into the mud, stopping the water; they are trying to suck up a little moisture from shallow puddles. We dig out the hose, pile rocks around it for protection, and stand watching as the water begins to fill the tank and the cows crowd in to drink. These are leftovers: cattle that for some reason weren't taken over east with the main herd. Eight yearling heifers are spending the summer with a young black Angus bull so their first calves will be small. Two big steers that were sore-footed when we sold the main bunch of calves are better now, fattening up. We're keeping the old cow with the cancerous eye close so we can wean her calf if she dies. Three cows out of cycle with the rest of the herd will calve soon.

A more "efficient" ranching operation probably would have sold these cattle immediately and written off any loss. By caring for them, we're taking an extra risk. We may lose; they may sell for less later.

We're keeping close watch on the cows that will calve soon, since Mike, who lives with his mother during the school year, usually misses out on that ritual of early spring. Lately he has excused low grades by expressing a desire to be a rancher when he grows up, and we want him to participate in the bloody rites of birth before he makes up his mind. We wish, with a touch of mischievousness, that we could arrange for him to be involved in calf-pulling as well, or maybe a calf born backward. His grades might shoot up dramatically. On the other hand, maybe not. He's already been bloodied by helping us brand, castrate and butcher, so gore-encrusted hard labor may not be discouraging.

I have always been enthusiastic about the values to be learned on a ranch. And not just the clichés about hard work. Last spring we pulled a big Charolais-cross calf that must have been premature, because he wouldn't suck by himself at first. The cow was reasonably quiet, but I spent hours bent over, head against her side, the fingers of one hand inside the calf's mouth while I tried to pump milk down him with the other. When I couldn't straighten up any more, and both arms were sticky with milk to the elbow, I'd milk the cow into the calf bucket, stick the rubber teat in his mouth and pump milk into him that way for a while.

This process continued three or four times a day for a week. Somewhere in the middle of the week the calf could hardly get up, his eyes had begun to sink back into his head, and the cow became irritable enough to kick at me, to kick the milk bucket over, to kick the calf. I got mad at both of them and began kicking the cow back, yelling at her, and prying the calf's mouth open with more force than was really necessary. George reminded me that the calf's mouth was probably sore, and I tried to be calm and gentle. I knew force doesn't work on animals. My father always reminds me, when I lose my temper, that it pays to be smarter than the cow. So I changed my attitude. I named the calf Rambo (because he was very large, but very stupid) and talked gently to him as I would to a small child. Suddenly he began to suck, his little tail switching back and forth like a pump handle; his eyes brightened, his belly rounded.

That's the kind of thing Mike could learn during calving season. I've come to believe force doesn't work well with the land, either.

First Gate:
Bovine Maneuvers

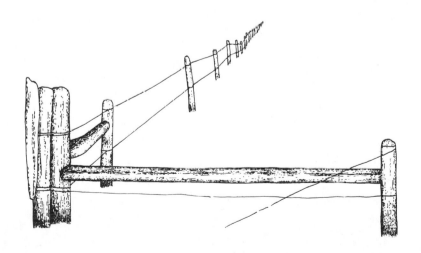

We get back into the hot truck and go through an open gate into my uncle's field, past an oat crop the neighbors put in for him this year. Because of the drought and a plague of grasshoppers, it has already been cut and stacked for hay instead of harvested. This is the second year they've lost the crop, though the oat hay will provide some return. But it won't be enough to repay the days they spent with their tractors plowing the field, dragging it to break up the big clods, piling larger rocks along the fence line.

So much for the hours of planting the oats under the hot April sun with dust billowing a hundred feet in the air. So much; so little.

We've watched this cycle, and participated in it. Yes, we can get good crops by plowing the bottom lands, but often the rain stops and we watch the topsoil blow away, the crop wither and dry up. We need the hay; if we get a successful oat crop, it can save us money wintering calves. But with conditions so harsh, oats or any non-native crop need a lot of help. Radio and TV programs are interrupted every few minutes in spring with ads for herbicides that will "get rid of quackgrass, bindweed" and other pests—but those pests grow primarily where the ground has been frequently plowed.

Each time we plow and don't get enough rain, and I watch the soil dry out and blow away, I think about some of the alternatives. In some areas, scientists are experimenting with perennial crops—plant them once and forget them. Think of the financial costs eliminated: repeated plowing, yearly fertilizing, yearly chemical applications, yearly machinery expenses. Not to mention the less tangible costs: compaction of the earth, the time spent. Our need for huge tractors would dwindle; farming truly would be revolutionized and be open to more people.

We also wonder about raising leaner cattle that have eaten no grain, nothing but native grass, a renewable resource. That's what we eat when we butcher our own cattle, and guests often remark upon its flavor and texture. Sometimes we explain why it's different from the soft, corn-fed beef they find in the supermarket.

Dust rises behind the tires; grasshoppers click against the windshield, blunder into the cab, cling to our collars and arms. Mike has given up tearing off one wing, and simply brushes them off. Yesterday, on my way home from town, I followed a pickup that zigzagged all over the highway, but I recognized the driver and was pretty sure he wasn't drunk. A few miles from home I realized he was swerving to run over grasshoppers—only a gesture, perhaps, but a symbolic one.

The truck bounces past an old water tank and windmill, idle now. The water level dropped a few years ago as demand increased with population. This tank and one a half-mile away, on the other side of the railroad tracks, are supplied from the same aquifer, and we chose to use the other. We carried the wheel from the windmill up onto a small hill near the house that acts as a storage place for broken machinery that may be of use someday—or may simply sit there and rust indefinitely.

First Gate

My father jokes, a little grimly, that people will ask "Why did he keep all this old junk?" when they attend his auction, but he often finds a part in his scrap pile that saves him buying a new one, and saves us a little hard cash. He is firmly convinced, not that taking care of small things will mean the big things take care of themselves, but that taking care of small things will give him the margin to survive.

He knows that the real sadness of an auction, which usually follows the death of a ranch owner, is that heirs are trying to get enough money to pay the huge inheritance taxes, or the debts. The fact that my mother and I have spent most of our lives here working to make this ranch succeed will not save us from inheritance taxes that may mean we have to sell half the ranch to pay them. And with only half the land, we probably wouldn't make enough money to break even.

On the top of my father's junk hill is an amazing assortment of stuff: a sprayer he bought at a military sale, several mowers we've cannibalized to repair the one we use, and a horse-drawn grader we hitch to the tractor to grade the road. Ours used to be a county road, but I spent five winters here alone before I married, and the county's policy is to plow only roads where two families live. Angry at being snowed in for two weeks one January, I posted a No Trespassing sign at the highway, and we maintain the road ourselves now. Father said it had been twenty years since the county graveled it, anyway. So one summer he did it himself by trading water to a highway construction crew in exchange for forty truckloads of gravel. Unfortunately, we're now charged fifty dollars an hour when shoveling snowdrifts is no longer enough to open a trail and we have to hire the county grader to open our road.

The storage area and junkyard is also a hay yard, where we move stacks in the fall. Some of the tall, gray ones beside the old horse-drawn mower have been waiting ten years or more to be used, and will still be green inside. They might be a metaphor for the junk he has kept, or for a rancher himself: though they look old and gray, they're full of useful life.

We detour into the dike pasture to dump our garbage in an old homesteader's cellar we are recycling for that purpose. (Each pasture has a specific designation. When one of us goes out alone, we leave a note, so if we don't come back the others will know where to look.) George picks up a beer bottle from beside a rock to toss it into the dump, then stops and holds it to his eye, laughs and passes it to me. Inside is a quaking mouse. Gently, we replace the bottle.

Remembering, we tell Mike about some trouble we had in this pasture with an old black whiteface cow named for a race horse. We called her Whirlaway because she was fast and suspicious. Whenever we moved the cattle anywhere, she ran in the opposite direction. If she had a calf, it galloped along in her wake, tail straight in the air just like Mama's, eyeballs rolling white.

We knew she'd be trouble when we gathered cows for fall sale. I eased the horse along behind the little bunch of cattle, paying no attention to her. If all the other cattle moved ahead of the horse, she would probably follow.

The cattle were still calm when we got to the gate George had opened. Quietly, I maneuvered the horse among the cows, gently cutting out the ones to be sold and moving them through the gate. Whenever you see a "cowboy" thundering along behind a herd of cattle, yelling and swinging his rope, he's either in a movie or he doesn't own the cows. Anyone who does that with real cows is losing money—they can run off hundreds of pounds of salable fat on a hot day.

Finally, every cow we wanted to sell was grazing quietly outside the gate—except Whirlaway. She stood beside the fence, head up, alert. I walked the horse her way as though going for a quiet Sunday ride.

She threw her head and tail up and trotted around me to join the group of cattle we planned to leave in the pasture. I kept calm. New tactic. I gathered the bunch and began to drive them all toward the gate. It would be extra trouble, because then we'd have to cut back the ones we didn't want, but worth it if she'd follow them quietly.

She wouldn't. She got right to the gate and ducked aside. We tried this maneuver several times, until my horse was wet with sweat. Once I got close behind her right at the gate and whooped. She raised her tail and shot out a stream of used grass, splashing green all over my horse's chest. This annoyed him. He snarled and opened his mouth to bite her on the hip. She raised her tail. He reconsidered, and his mouth snapped shut, teeth clattering.

I decided to use another tactic that sometimes works: tiring her out. Trotting the horse, I simply followed her wherever she wanted to go, back and forth on the flat—fortunately free of prairie-dog holes. Each time she got close to the gate I'd try to cut her toward it.

My horse is a beautiful, gray part-Arab with a rocking, easy gait. But he's lazy; he gets along with as little work as possible. Only when he's really angry, hot and tired does he turn into the cutting horse his sainted mother, Rebel, was, slashing back and forth behind the cow, anticipating every move she makes, crowding her with his chest and teeth until she has no choice. Half an hour of trotting behind Whirlaway made him mad, and he went to work. The long fall grass was slick and treacherous. Each time he made a tight turn—one of those where he was almost horizontal to the ground—I seemed to feel a broken leg coming on. But he never made a misstep.

Then she kicked him in the chest. He gasped, snorted and bit her tail. She kicked again, just as he turned, and one back hoof connected with my knee, the other with my ankle. I was absolutely sure the ankle was broken. The pain was intense, but the leg got numb after a few minutes. I was angry. I kicked the horse into a gallop, and we went after her again.

The cow made a wide circle down into a gully, then up the side. The horse was right behind her. When she reached the top, she suddenly turned, and roared down the hill, smashing her head against the horse's chest and lifting him from the ground. By this time I was yelling words that probably originated with the first cowboy, somewhere in the deserts of the Middle East or the steppes of Asia. The horse slid sideways and she hurtled past. I've seen lots of bovine maneuvers, but never a cow clever enough to try to tip a horse over.

My husband was getting annoyed with Whirlaway by this time, and came roaring up to her in the pickup, with the horse and me on the other side. She immediately took to rough country, forcing the pickup to go around. The horse and I followed her, trotting steadily.

When the pickup caught up with us, we began alternating in driving her. When she got ahead of me, George would turn her with the truck, and then I'd haze her along while he caught up. Posts, baling wire, fence stretchers and the usual collection of junk hung suspended above the bed of the pickup as it bounced from rock to rock, billowing black exhaust. Whirlaway kicked the pickup; she swung her head and smashed in a door panel. Once, with George behind and me trying to turn her, she dashed straight into a barbed wire fence. The next time she hit the truck, she smeared blood from the barbed wire cuts along the door.

Finally Whirlaway slowed down, turned and plodded steadily almost two miles back to the gate. All of us were running with sweat. The next day she seemed to have recovered completely.

No, we weren't torturing her unnecessarily. She

was old and dry; she wouldn't calve the next year. She had to go, and if we'd let her get away we'd have had to do the same thing all over again. Not all cows are this hard to corral, but a half-day like this isn't really unusual in the cattle business, either. Whenever a city friend envies us the ranching life, and says "all you have to do is sit around and watch those cows get fat," I think of Whirlaway. And I don't think too badly of her. She was just being a cow.

Mike wrinkles his nose at the smell from the boneyard, where we dragged last winter's failures: cows that simply froze to death after two months of nights when the thermometer never got above zero. But he's fascinated by the shapes visible above the blowing grass. I needed to visit here anyway; I owe some bones to a friend. Not long ago I met Emma, a tiny Native American woman who makes and sells dolls in the image and clothing of her ancestors, with beaded buckskin dresses, moccasins and blanket leggings—every detail correct. The craft sprang out of her childhood, when her mother made what they called "pieces" dolls, small stuffed heads with cotton material gathered at the neck for dresses, and no bodies. The dolls have no faces, Emma told me, because her mother was apprehensive about accidentally portraying a real person and bringing them bad luck, and also so Emma could imagine the doll's mood to be anything she liked. Emma's dolls come in several sizes and are owned by collectors all over the country. Occasionally she makes a man on a horse drawing a travois carrying a woman. The horses, she explained, she collects rather than makes. Originally, Indian children used a bone from the hoofs of buffalo that resembled a horse enough for the imaginative; when the buffalo disappeared, they began using a similar bone from cows' hoofs. But Emma can't always find the bones she needs, so I have decided to take some to her as a gift for the story of the dolls.

While I'm looking for hoofs, I think about that adaptation. The buffalo disappeared with the old ways, so the children found cow bones that would work for their play, hitched the horses to sardine cans to imitate wagons. Emma and her brother would build tiny corrals, and each would pretend to have a ranch. "Then he'd always want to have a prairie fire, and it was always my ranch that got burned out," she recalled, smiling. Thirty years earlier, her own mother had played as a child with buffalo hoofs; seventy years later, Emma makes dolls snatched up by people eager for some token of the way the past was. When nature no longer supplied the buffalo bones, the Indians found something else to use. One can't build too much on this slender fact, but it seems to me symbolic in an important way of differing views of the world: the Indians adapted to nature; white men try to make nature adapt to their desires.

Mike has walked through the coyote-gnawed bones and found a cow carcass with a small skull still tucked behind the ribs. He takes along several long rib bones, slashing the air with them as if they were knives or swords.

I realize suddenly that the circle of our world lies within a mile radius. Here lie our homes, the garden whose products supplement our own beef to feed our bodies, the wintering and birthing grounds for our cattle, the hayfields that feed them, the boneyard where they slowly return to earth, the junkyard where dead machinery becomes spare parts, and the garbage dump where we get rid of what we cannot use. All that is missing is a graveyard for the humans; it may not be too late.

I think of our lives as circular: our work is dedicated not just to profit-making but literally to feeding ourselves. We are sometimes able to choose work that sustains us mentally, or at least gives us variety, and to plan our own days rather than working to a schedule set up by someone else. But the steady rhythm of night turning to day, spring to summer, birth to death, the progress of the moon and sun, the sweep of wind and rain—those natural cycles determine how we arrange our lives. What does not fit into the smooth circle of our days, into the repeating cycle of the seasons, does not belong here.

Second Gate:
Wintering

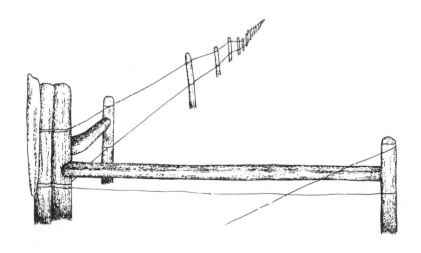

*W*e turn east and open the gate at the railroad tracks about a mile from the house. Most of the other gates we've gone through, into alfalfa fields, have been open; they're closed only when lack of feed makes us turn cattle into the fields in winter, or when we're moving cows.

Mike's thirsty already, and goes to the back of the truck for the water jug. While we wait we automatically pick up pop cans that could cut a cow's hoof. We never throw even a gum wrapper in the pasture; the cans were tossed away by the last railroad crew that passed desultorily through. They apparently make some effort to maintain the roadbed, but the fence sags as it has for forty years; the only repairs have been ours.

Another problem we have with the railroad is the habit its trains have of setting fires; sparks fly either from a hotbox or from the engine into the high grass along the tracks. The fire departments in our area are all volunteer—anyone who can grab a shovel fights fires. But by the time someone along the track sees smoke and calls the fire department and the neighbors, the flames often have a head start.

We cross the tracks and drive past the old Lindsay place, where John and Anna lived until they sold out to my father and moved to Hermosa. After that, John emulated other retired ranchers and didn't live long. Their widows may live on to cheery old age, crocheting potholders for the church bazaars, helping with the pancake suppers, judging cakes at the county fair. But when old ranchers are deprived of their cows and their work, they bend, stoop and lie down to sink into the earth.

I remember visiting the Lindsay house as a child. It had been deserted for some time; the chrome-trimmed, black wood stove still stood in a corner of the kitchen, but the wallpaper was peeling. I crept up the narrow stairs to the two rooms above. Mice had built nests from mattress stuffing in the corners, and white mounds of bird manure lay below the windowsills in the bedrooms.

Even then I felt it was wrong for the house to be empty when a family could have made it home. When John and Anna were married, it was possible to make a living on a couple of hundred acres, if everyone worked hard enough and did what is now called "diversification." The ranch wife and kids usually maintained a big garden, enough chickens to provide meat, and eggs to eat and sell, possibly pigs or a few bees for extra income. But almost no one keeps chickens or pigs these days, or rears enough children to take care of these diverse chores. The prevailing wisdom is that a family can't make a living on such a small acreage—another aspect of the monoculture that has spread even to the plains.

A few years ago, before television, inhabitants of many regions of the country were largely unaware of their differences from the metropolitan population, the setters of style. When we began to notice that not everyone wore leather belts with names carved into the back, or put black bandanas around their necks, we were proud of our differences at first. Only gradually did we

---

begin to abhor our own uniqueness. "Redneck" had been a simple description of what happens when a person wears an open-necked shirt and works outside; it became a term of derision for others to use against us, a term that caused fists to be clenched if we heard it. Now we throng the shopping malls, buying sleazy, impractical clothing because it's in fashion; our speech is losing its color and spice as we adopt the slang popular on programs that invade the majority of living rooms in the nation. Even in South Dakota, restaurants serve "Cajun" food with almost as much frequency as they serve steak and potatoes. You still must search long and hard for any authentic aspect of the food or culture of the pioneers, or the Native Americans who preceded them.

If, instead of aping whichever area is the site of the latest popular television show, each region concentrated on its own strengths, we'd have a considerably different—and more efficient—country. Bioregionalism, it's called, and I've read enough about it to become enthusiastic, but the word hasn't exactly passed into everyday usage. The idea is this: each biological region of a country would look first at what it could produce and make at home (assuming all imports ceased). Instead of all of us living in frame houses, we'd diversify. Native southwesterners learned to use adobe because it held heat in winter and was cool in summer; we northern plains dwellers could make wide use of underground houses, earth-baffled against frigid winter temperatures but open to the sun that often shines. Instead of drawing electricity from scarce water supplies, or building nuclear power plants with millions in government subsidies, we'd build wind generators to utilize the power of the wind that scours the prairie every day. And if we couldn't make something, we'd do without it—an idea pioneers like the Lindsays wouldn't find strange at all.

When we bought the Lindsay place we tore the house down for lumber, except for the kitchen, which we recycled. We hauled it home, put a fourth wall on it and used it for a bunkhouse. Our various hired men seemed happy in its primitive elegance, with a round Warm Morning wood stove, a dresser with an enamel washbasin, dipper and pail, a shelf for personal items. Now, though, twenty years later, no self-respecting hired man could put up with a wood-burning stove, but thousands of city people can't wait to move "back to the land" and get one.

When I married for the first time, my husband's three children visited us in the summers. We lived in a small apartment attached to my parents' house, and summer crowded it considerably. So I repainted the bunkhouse inside and out and put down scraps of linoleum; then the children had their own summer house. After the marriage dissolved and the children stopped visiting, I turned the bunkhouse into a workroom for my press. It was stacked to the eaves with the books I published and decorated with pages from the magazine I printed for a while. Through all these transformations, it has remained "the bunkhouse." I often wonder if the spirit of the house, or of Anna who spent so much time in it, appreciates its continued, loving use.

Second Gate

John Lindsay's barn is still there, a once-red, wood-shingled structure where he kept his cows in the historic winter of 1949, still spoken of with awe in these parts. We regularly have what one ranching woman in Wyoming calls the "annual going-out-of-business blizzard," when a rancher who has several hundred head of cattle or sheep one day may have lost most of them three days later. In 1949, when John struggled to the barn after the three-day blizzard and pried the door open, he found it full of snow and live cows. The cows had kept moving around, tramping the snow down, until their backs were against the roof. When he opened the door, they tumbled down into the corral, healthy but a little cramped. Hundreds of cows—depending on whose estimate you accept—died in that blizzard.

The county road grader got stuck in our yard early in the storm and remained there for a month. Dad had just bought his new Chevrolet pickup, gone to a New Year's Eve dance in Hermosa, and stopped at my uncle Harold's place on the way home. He came back across the pasture with the sky clear and full of stars about 3:00 A.M. Tired, he left the pickup in the yard instead of putting it in the garage. By breakfast, which I suppose was around 6:00, the snow was two feet deep and drifting. By the time he finished his coffee, the pickup was stuck where it would remain for a month.

Luckily, he still had the team of Belgians, Bud and Beauty, and wherever they could go, he hauled hay to feed the cattle. I am lucky enough to remember the horses blowing and warm in the darkness of the barn.

_____

While he put on the harnesses, Father told me stories about other men and their teams.

One of the early residents used to break a team by tying two wild workhorses to a couple of good posts in the corral. He'd hobble them if he had to, and then he'd put the rigging on, hitch the wagon, take off the hobbles and open the corral gate. Then he'd get up in the wagon and have somebody untie them. By the time he got to town, he had a broke team, and was ready for a drink.

The same man had a runaway one day when his wife and baby daughter were in the wagon. Without a second's hesitation, he tossed the reins to his wife, grabbed the baby and jumped out. His wife drove the team home. Community intelligence is silent on what the couple discussed next.

I cherish these stories. Back then a real relationship could exist between a man and a horse. Today, we try to recapture the feeling by naming our cars, but it's not the same.

During the Blizzard of '49, when the snow was so deep even the team couldn't drag a loaded hayrack through it, Father rode his big sorrel gelding, Zarro, hauling protein cake across the back of the saddle as the horse struggled and plunged through the drifts. We still use a saddle horse to feed when the trucks and tractors are stuck or won't start. The Winter of '85, for instance, lasted six months and broke every record in the book.

Some ranchers put all their cattle in corrals at the home place during winter, with heated or at least

---

flowing water in tanks, and feed handy to be distributed by tractors. My father knows, after seventy years' experience, that smaller bunches of cattle do better if they are free to graze in the pasture. With less crowding, the weaker and smaller animals get more feed, and when the snow melts, all the cattle can supplement their diet with grass they find themselves. It occurs to me that the same rule might apply to humans, who crowd together in larger and larger cities, until the weak and ill must be supported by ever-greater public contributions.

Cattle are also healthier if they get native grasses in the winter, since the grass contains nutrients not present, or not ample enough, in prepared feeds. In 1985, when our cattle couldn't leave the corrals for two months because of snow depths, they gnawed on the planks, sounding like a herd of chain saws. None of the expensive minerals we tried stopped the chewing; when the snow melted and they could get grass again, they stopped just in time to save our corrals.

In spite of the fact that it's more work for us and more risk for the cattle, we also enjoy leaving them in the pastures as long as possible. Cattle wandering the prairie are more like wild animals, freer and more noble than the pitiful creatures cooped up miserably with their own excrement sucking at their ankles in a feed lot. When the snow gets so deep we can't get to them with a truck, we're forced to bring them closer to the feed. At a time like that, it always seems to me that even nonreligious ranchers consciously avoid any possible blasphemy. They'll pause in their work, look up at the snow-laden sky, and say mildly, "We need the moisture, but I wouldn't mind if this would stop now."

However, water becomes a major problem when cattle remain free in pastures during the winter. Most of our water is stored in man-made dams, covered in winter with ice which must be chopped with an axe before the cattle can drink. Only after the ice gets more than a foot thick, or the snow gets so deep we can't get to the pasture at all, do we give up ice-chopping and bring the cattle closer to home and the water tanks.

Chopping ice is an acquired skill. My first swing always bounces the axe off the ice, so I have to take a deep breath and start over. The axe-wielder stands with feet spread, balances, inhales and lets the axe fall straight toward the ice. The axe bites cleanly into the ice an inch or two, again and again, until it has carved a line a foot or more long. Then he—or she—pivots and chops until a square hole is outlined. With a few more strokes, the hole is opened, and the water gurgles up to fill it. With each stroke of the axe, the water sprays up, instantly freezing onto coveralls at thirty below zero. When the hole is clear, the process is repeated a few feet away until the cattle can drink at several holes without crowding.

One cold December day we found a duck swimming frantically in a hole he'd kept open all night with his efforts. We sprinkled oats on the shore nearby. But the next morning the duck was gone—either south or into the gullet of a coyote. We'll never know.

Second Gate

If the winter is comparatively open and warm, we may chop five to ten holes in a dam every day from November through March or early April. Most of our neighbors now have covered tanks for winter use, so they don't have to chop ice. I tell them we're the only real ranchers left. They think I'm kidding.

Third Gate:
Shade for the Prancing Horse

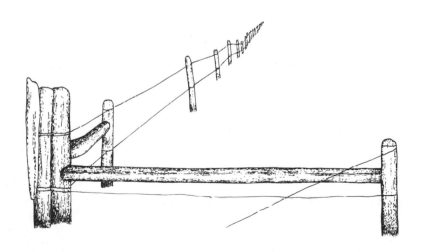

P ast the Lindsay buildings, we turn south against the hot sun glare, past another alfalfa field that hasn't produced much this year. The deserted buildings stand at one end of it, and Mike wants to explore them, but we don't have time. To distract him, I tell him another story, about the land nearer town where our best hay-fields are, and where our cattle winter.

My father says he and his two brothers were haying down there with teams of horses when Lucky Lindbergh went over. He dipped his wings as he went over the town, and landed in Rapid City. They'd read in the paper he'd be coming over, and just happened to be off the teams and looking around when they heard the plane. They realized, as they watched it and listened to the horses stamp their feet that an era had ended.

Often when they were haying there, a family that lived south of town would go by—father, mother and their retarded son. The family—I'll call them Jones—raised watermelons on their tiny irrigated place, and they'd often stop to sell one to the men haying. No such sale can be politely accomplished without conversation, and the Hasselstrom brothers would always ask how Mr. Jones was. He'd say, "Mentally, we're doing all right, but physically we're not so good." Sometimes he'd say, "Physically, we're doing all right, but mentally we're not so good." His wife never said anything, just sat on the wagon seat looking straight ahead, while the boy petted the team of horses. As the years went by, the couple grew older and more bent, their son grew middle-aged but no smarter, and the community wondered what would happen.

Then one day the three brothers were cutting a second crop, when Mr. Jones's team came running down the road. He was lashing them with the reins and shouting about his son being lost. One brother kept stacking and the other two caught saddle horses and rode on out to the Jones place, while Mr. Jones went to town for more help. Mrs. Jones was standing in the yard when they arrived, and she spoke to them as if she had an education and refinement, telling them the Jones buildings had already been searched. ("Imagine that," said the storyteller, "that little woman living there all those years with those two men, neither of them right in the head.") The neighbors hunted most of the day before someone happened to think of the root cellar on the deserted homestead a mile away. By that time it had grown dark, so they took a lantern along, and one of the brothers, stooping, took it into the cellar. The son was there, hanging from a rafter.

Mike shivers, and notices we're in the prairie dog town. It's grown to about ten acres, including a rich, wet bottom that would grow alfalfa if it weren't for the dogs. They eat the plants and roots in spoke-shaped patterns around their holes, leaving the ground bare for perhaps twenty feet around each one. The dens are collared with mud pressed together until it's as firm as adobe; it serves as protection and sunshade. The dogs are piping now, standing up on their hind legs, dropping down, running in circles with tails twitching furiously, warning each other of our approach. Mike is already reaching for the pistol. He knows I hate the dogs' damage enough to let him shoot any he can hit.

George leans out the window and takes a few shots; Mike collects the spent cartridges and whistles through them, trying to imitate the dogs. The burrowing owls that live in abandoned prairie dog holes take nervous flight and perch on fence posts out of the line of fire. I've loved and protected the owls since, riding at dusk across the dog town, I heard an imperious *WHOOO!* that seemed to come from the right hoof of my horse. I looked down. Just to the right sat a shape that reached barely three inches to his fetlock. It looked up at me with eyes reflecting moonlight, and demanded again, *WHO!*, in a tone that suggested irritation. I apologized out loud and watched the horse's feet more carefully.

Mike has heard my lecture before, but listens to my grumbling. When a prairie dog town gets this large, it destroys pasture and endangers cattle and horses by harboring rattlesnakes as well as creating leg-breaking traps. Some of my most heated discussions with other environmentalists involve the prairie dogs. I don't believe any species should be wiped out, but I also don't believe the average environmentalist has ever had to chase a cow on horseback through a prairie dog town. Only survivors of the job should speak to the problem.

Two years ago we decided to cut the population of this town. I had long argued against poison, both for the burrowing owls' sake and because of the danger to the other wildlife, which might eat a poisoned dog and pass the death along. We considered buying a pair of ferrets, but were told tame ones have lost their instinct to hunt. So we bought prairie dog bombs, cardboard cylinders about three inches long containing phosphorus. The theory is that as they burn they exhaust the oxygen in the hole and suffocate the dogs.

With each supply of bombs come little plastic packages of fuses two to four inches long. We put the bombs on the tailgate of the pickup, punch holes in one end of each bomb with a jackknife and stick in a fuse. When enough are ready, we load the prepared bombs into a shoulder sack, fill our pockets with matches and grab a shovel. One of us lights a fuse and drops the bomb into the hole. The other shovels dirt to cover the entrance before the bomb begins to burn.

Several things affect the efficiency of this method. For one, the fuse sometimes burns instantly and, if the bomb isn't in the hole, it sets a grass fire. Second, sometimes we can a hear bomb rolling three minutes later, down a hole that may be thirty, forty, fifty feet long. Third, a hole can be two feet in diameter and drop five feet straight down before bending; in the seconds before the bomb ignites, try filling that space with dry prairie earth on which no rain has fallen for two months.

To speed the bombs down the holes, we take a short length of plastic pipe and drop them into that. Once, a bomb stuck in the pipe, so we shoveled dirt over the end of it; when we pulled it back, the end of the pipe was a mass of melted plastic. This led to a discussion of the guerrilla potential of prairie dog bombs; legal, safe and easy to hide, they may be one of the most efficient incendiary devices ever made. We joked about using them on offensive structures from railroad bridges to bulldozers to uranium exploration vehicles. All fantasy.

The first summer we tried to wipe out the prairie dog town, we put a thousand bombs into that ten acres without ever hitting the same hole twice. The second summer, on a series of days when the temperature was over a hundred degrees, we used another fifteen hundred bombs.

Mike made the world's largest collection of prairie dog skulls, teeth, tiny shoulder bones, leg bones, fingers. I made a mobile of ribs to hang in the window; they click together gently when the wind blows, reminding me not so much of death as of the tenacity of life. The prairie dogs still have a vigorous population, and whistle mockingly at us when we drive past.

But they're hiding now, and we have work to do. Mike has noticed my mention of the wasted grass, and asks how big this pasture is, starting me on another lecture. If I told him the pasture held several hundred acres, he wouldn't be any wiser; I need to make some analogy. Cattlemen here figure it takes forty acres to feed a cow unit, consisting of a cow and calf.

Few of the old-time ranchers will tell you how many cattle they have, let alone how many acres of land they own or lease. Even ranchers who have known each other for fifty years, and who may know to the penny how much everyone in the county pays in taxes, will not tell one another the amount of their holdings in land or cattle. When some visitor asks my law-abiding Republican father, he gets a faraway look in his eye, smiles in a friendly manner—and lies.

Ranchers consider such a question to be similar to my asking a store owner, "How much money do you have in the bank?" It's simply not done. While ranchers might honestly answer an impertinent question about religion or politics, they feel no compunction about lying when the answer would give the questioner a clue to their net worth. That's private. I know some who won't even tell the government when giving specifics would result in rebates or subsidies. They would rather take off their clothes on the steps of the church.

So Mike is still wondering how big the pasture is, and how much land my father owns.

We pass the scattered remains of Lumpjaw, a cow who probably had bone cancer. Her jaw swelled enormously, but we wanted her to raise her calf. Instead she fell into the water tank and froze solid one night. It is quite difficult to get a frozen cow out of a water tank surrounded by eight-foot snowdrifts, even with a four-wheel-drive pickup. She had her revenge.

I don't know why, but when we retire horses, they often spend their last days in this pasture. When my father got his tractor and turned the team out, this is where they lived. Every year he'd think we might need them, but every year they'd spend the summer grazing, and run off if we got too close. Once in a while he'd get

---

the tractor stuck in a snowdrift and then would hitch the team up, and when they pulled it out he'd say, "You can't beat a team!" But mostly they grazed, and shied away if I tried to get close to them. I was back from college and we were standing by the corral fence, looking at my pregnant mare, when my father told me that Beauty had died. He had sold Bud. I think he did it so that the old gelding, who had run and worked with Beauty for twenty years, wouldn't be lonely.

My mare foaled a filly, and I named her Beauty. The mare was half-Arab, and the filly was sired by a registered stallion, so I registered the filly and got back papers decorated with scrollwork with her name outlined in gold. I gave them to my father.

I had learned to ride while breaking my first mare, so I went to work right away on the filly. I spent the summer petting her, feeding her, getting her used to my hands and to a halter. The mare, Ginger, was quiet and gentle, but Beauty was wild from the first. Day after day I'd bring the mare into the corral and then walk to the filly with her halter, speaking quietly, soothingly. Some times she'd stand quietly while I haltered her and led her around; other times she'd suddenly whirl and kick at me. Once she caught my arm just above the elbow when I threw it up to protect my head; it was numb for hours. My father began to get worried, and came with me every day when I worked Beauty.

We always picketed our horses when they were young, to get them used to being tied. We'd try them out in the corral first, so they wouldn't be hurt, tying the long rope through the halter and then onto some heavy object like a telephone pole.

But when we tried it with Beauty, though she'd been tied often, she always stood trembling for a moment and then ran. When she reached the end of the rope, she'd flip over and land heavily on her side. Most horses, if they do run on a picket rope, will flip themselves once or twice, learn a valuable lesson about ropes, and never do it again. Beauty would do it over and over for hours, until her head was bloody and her sides heaved. I'd cry and speak gently to her, and lead her to the end of the rope so she could feel that it was taut; nothing seemed to help. Finally we'd take her off it and turn her back out with her mother.

But my father would say, "She's got to learn that. If she won't respect a rope, you won't ever be able to trust her when she's old enough to ride."

When I came back from college the next spring, I went straight to the corral. Beauty was a big yearling, and beautiful, her sorrel mane and tail streaked with blond. But when I walked up to her, she snorted, whirled and kicked straight for my head. I threw myself backward and, while I was dusting myself off, she came at me, ears back, sharp little hoofs reaching for me. I scrambled over the fence and fell into my father's arms. He steadied me, then said, "She does that all the time. I've worked with her all winter, every day." He looked worried; his blue eyes squinted against the sun.

"I've never hit her, even when I wanted to. I've always talked quiet to her and been as gentle as I could.

But I kept tying her up; she's got to learn if she's going to be any good."

We stood outside the corral and watched her. He was afraid I'd think he'd been rough on her, and kept repeating that he'd never hurt her.

"But she hurts herself all the time. Look at her head." It was covered with scabs. "Every time I get near her she either runs straight into the corral fence, or comes after me like that. I've never seen a horse act like that; it's like she's crazy. You know, we've raised work-horses since I was a kid, and I've just never seen anything like this."

For the next two days I worked with her my-self—under Father's strict orders not to go near her unless he was close by. And she was crazy. Nothing I could do would calm her. One time she'd run from me, run straight into the high board fence as if she didn't see it, and fall down, scratched and bloody. The next day she'd turn on me, and bite and kick at me, until I dashed for the fence. There seemed to be no pattern, no reason.

Three days after I got home, we branded, and the neighbors came to help. When we stopped for dinner and headed back to the house, their daughter looked over at the small corral that held Beauty.

"What a beautiful filly! Are you breaking her?"

"We're trying. She really acts strange."

We walked to the corral fence and climbed up, watching her. She stood in the far corner, snorting. Suddenly she ran at us, and we jumped off the fence. She ran straight into it, fell back, and stood up shaking.

"Is she blind?"

"No, we've thought of that. But she does that kind of thing all the time."

During dinner, all the girl could talk of was Beauty. It was plain that she thought we'd mistreated her, and that she could do better. She offered us a hundred dollars for her, then a hundred-fifty. My father said no, that we wanted her ourselves.

But at supper, after the neighbors had gone home, he said, "You know, we have to decide what to do about that colt. I sure don't want to sell her to Kathy; she might get killed. But I don't think there's any use in working with her any longer. One of us could get hurt, and there's no sense in that."

"Can we take her to the sale ring?" I asked.

"Well, how would you feel if somebody else bought her and they got hurt? I'd hate to think we made money off her, and then she killed somebody. And she could; if I wasn't watching her all the time she'd have got me this winter. Someone else might not be so gentle with her, either."

We sat for a long time, looking out the window.

"But what can you do?" asked my mother, pouring more coffee.

"Well, I was wondering how my daughter would feel if she just disappeared some day."

"You mean shoot her?" I asked, full of young bluntness.

"Yes," he said without hesitation, and looked at me. He looked the way he had when he told me that old

Beauty had died. I cried in my bed that night. But in the morning I told him that if he felt that was best, I'd accept his judgment.

"Will you blame me for it?"

"No." I wasn't sure, but I had to say no.

When I went back to college, she was still in her corral. We fed and watered her, and occasionally I tried to explain things to her, but we'd stopped trying to work with her. She still threw herself either at the corral or at us whenever we came near.

I married and stayed away from the ranch for several years, teaching, working. My father never mentioned Beauty in his rare letters; both my old mares were alive and well, but he never bred Beauty's mother again. After my divorce, I came back to the ranch, built a two-room apartment onto my folks' house, and started trying to remember how to write stories and poems.

One day I was gathering cattle and rode down into a little hollow to get a cow that had calved there. The calf was new and tottery, so I got off my horse to help it along. The cow would run ahead a few steps, then turn back and moo, and the calf would stumble ahead, then stop, and I'd boost him along. I was enjoying the blue sky, the green grass, a cool breeze, when Ginger snorted and jumped aside.

I looked where she was staring, saw bones in the grass and went to look closer. There was a shoulder bone, a leg bone gnawed by coyotes. And then the head: a small horse's skull, with a little hole in the center of the forehead. Beauty.

I turned the skull over with my boot and saw a little triangular head slip out of an eyehole, then the flicker as a rattlesnake coiled himself where the skull had been. He was a baby, but wrapped neatly in three coils that would have fit in the palm of my hand. His little tail rattled and his black tongue flickered in and out as his head swung back and forth, testing the air, wondering whether to glide away or to strike.

Somewhere in this pasture an old mare stands, probably switching flies in the shade of the only tree, a cedar. She's Beauty's grandmother, my old Rebel, given to me as a yearling filly by my uncle Harold when I was eleven. My father and I couldn't catch her mother—few people ever had—so we put two ropes on Rebel's halter and attempted to lead her home between our horses. She reared, kicked, stamped, whinnied and fought the ropes like a wolverine.

The mare was even wilder. She was pure red, the red that set people who saw her to talking about prairie fires and sunsets. Her Arab ancestry showed in a delicate nose, her mane was long and tangled, her tail swept the ground when it wasn't carried straight in the air. She pranced around us, screaming and snorting, and the filly did her damnedest to break loose. I named her that day.

I already had a horse, an old fat mare named Blaze who I'd bought with eighty dollars of my own money and who had suited me quite well. Once I saw that filly, though, I realized my error.

Every day my father caught Rebel and tied her

in the barn to quiet her down. He told me never to get on her in there, because if she reared she'd squash my skull against the rafters. But as soon as he left, I'd slip out to the barn. I was a timid child, and probably spent at least one day talking to her before I got on her. But I had to keep my head down, and that's no position for an Indian princess or whatever I was pretending to be at the time.

I'm still not good at knots, and my father had used a bowline, which takes practice. I worked with a scrap of rope until I thought I could imitate the knot, then untied Rebel and led her to the corral. I got on her without a bridle because we didn't have one to fit her. She snorted, jumped a bit, but seemed to enjoy my attention. I rode her every day.

No doubt, since I couldn't really tie a bowline knot for another ten years, my father suspected what I was doing. But he didn't catch me for quite a while.

"How long have you been doing that?" he asked quietly from the barn door.

I hadn't heard him approach, and nearly fell off the horse. "Uh, quite a while."

"Been bucked off?"

"No, she hasn't even tried."

"Well, let's try the saddle."

He kept an eye on me after that, but I rode my Rebel every day from then on.

Once, at a rodeo in Hermosa, I cut across an open field in a show-off hurry to get to the parade, and rode her at a gallop into a tangle of barbed wire. She could have killed me. On top of that, most horses would have hurt or ruined themselves. But Rebel just stood there and looked at me with reproach.

The wire was over her head, around the saddle, around her legs. I had to hurt her to get her free, and it took time. A crowd gathered. Several ranchers suggested that I might as well shoot her; even my father was dubious, but he kept quiet. I kept talking to her, and crying, and she didn't move a muscle until I asked her to, lifting each leg delicately as I freed it. When it was over, I doctored her cuts and rode her in the parade.

For years I was the only person to ride her, and my love affair with her is the most perfect I've ever had. The others ended in heartbreak or marriage or both. She never betrayed me. She put up with my idiocies and idiosyncrasies. Every injury I got while riding her was my own fault, and I apologized to her each time.

Rebel is retired, the only horse in this pasture. She was a good cow horse; now she enjoys causing trouble when we round up cattle, chasing them in every direction but the right one. My father has threatened to sell her, but I plead her long years of service. When the time comes that she's ill or too thin in winter, I hope I have the courage to shoot her so she can die here where she loved to run. I won't send her to a packing plant. Of course, if we ran the ranch with the efficiency of the people who call ranching and farming "agribusiness," we'd sell her for dog food and buy a horse that would do us some good. Wasting pasture on an old horse doesn't make any money.

Third Gate

A favorite autumn pastime in this area is visiting the wildlife park in the Black Hills at night, with a thermos of kahlua-laced coffee and a package of sandwiches, to listen to the elk bugle during mating season. The experience is rare; the sound of the rutting elk practically indescribable. A few years ago a friend told me of hiking back toward her car in the dark after such an evening. Her group had no flashlight, since they'd forgotten one when they hiked up the hill in the afternoon, but the faint glow from a slender moon seemed to be reflected and augmented by the tall silvery grass underfoot. When she was ready to rest, she spotted what she thought was a large rock beside the path and dropped gratefully onto it. The rock grunted, and she was catapulted some distance either by her own terror, or by the rock, which stood up and shook itself. Even without a flashlight, she could tell by the bulk that she'd sat on a buffalo. Shaking, she backed away. She was lucky: the buffalo snorted in disgust and wandered off.

A buffalo can be as much as nine feet long, weigh up to a ton and stand six feet at the shoulder. Shortsighted but with a keen sense of smell, they are dangerous and unpredictable. Few years pass without a tourist ignoring Buffalo Are Dangerous signs and being gored or trampled in a national park near where we live. Ferocious in defense of their territory or young, buffalo can outrun most horses. Buffalo hide is so thick, ordinary bullets will pierce it only at thin spots, and the curved black horns are so sharp a buffalo can gut another with one swinging thrust of his head.

How could anyone sit on a buffalo, even in the dark? Why didn't some primitive instinct scream *Danger!* as she approached? Since I heard that story, I've practiced walking in utter darkness, trying to use all my senses to explore the world around me. The more I work at it, the better I get, but I'm still pitifully dependent on flashlights even on my own familiar hillside.

How far we have come from our origin as a part of the land; how far we are from truly mingling with and understanding our world. Our essential, primitive instincts have been switched off; our minds have been directed inward, analyzing our childhoods, fears, motives, needs. Probably all these things are important, but if we dive too deeply into our psyches and leave the natural world too far behind, we may never reach it again.

We have lost touch with our primitive instincts, so we can no longer sense the buffalo; for instinct, we have substituted a cold-hearted efficiency that has no time for an old horse.

Fourth Gate:
Wildlife Pasture

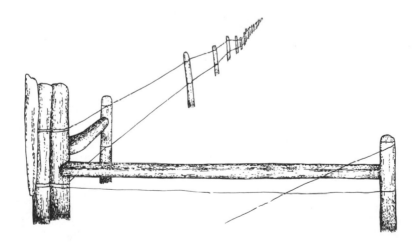

We come to the first of four pastures owned by other people that we cross to reach our own land again. This gate is a tight one, but my father made it easier for me years ago by putting a chain and nail in place of the wire loop that holds most wire gates in this country. The chain is long so almost anyone can get a loop over the nail, at least partially closing the gate.

The first time I saw pronghorn antelope we startled them coming over this hill. Four of them sprang under the barbed-wire fence so the wires sang. Deer jump fences; antelope run toward them at full speed, duck their heads to take the wire against their curved-back horns, and seem to spring under, snapping the wire back harmlessly after their hindquarters are safe. They can be on the other side of a fence with scarcely a break in stride faster than you can read this, running with their white rear-ends flashing comically. I've always looked upon them as one of the most primitive of the prairie species, perhaps because they don't eat grass but exist mostly on weeds and shrubs, even sagebrush, though most ranchers insist they'll eat alfalfa if they can get it. But historically, they fit nicely into the food chain, since they aren't really competing with the larger grazers.

Getting back in the truck, Mike sees a piece of cattle cake in the tool box and picks it up.

"What's this?" he asks, blue eyes solemn.

"Cake, Michael. We feed it to the cows in the winter when the grass is covered with snow."

"What's in it?"

"Ground corn, molasses, wheat." I keep my

face straight and glance at George. He grins. We both know what's coming next.

"Can people eat it?"

"Sure. We eat the same kinds of things. Cereal is corn and wheat."

Silence.

"Can I eat some of it?"

"Sure."

"Can I, Dad?" Kids usually hedge their bets.

"I don't care, son. You might like it."

"And it would be cheaper than the lobster you ordered in Cheyenne," I put in. I don't think children should be informed about lobster until they can pay for it themselves, but Mike learned early.

Mike looks at each of us carefully, familiar with our jokes. We keep our faces straight. He sticks the corner of the piece of cake in his mouth and crunches. Then he looks straight ahead, watching the horizon go by while he chews thoughtfully.

"How is it?" George asks innocently.

"Not bad," Mike answers with a blasé shrug. "Might be better with cream and sugar."

"Did I mention that it probably has rat poop in it?" George asks.

Mike's eyes widen. "It does?" he mutters, mouth full.

"Yeah," I add helpfully. "The rats get in the grain warehouses and then they just grind up everything. There might even be a whole rat in it." But he's already crawling across George's lap to spit out the window.

Between sputterings, he asks, "Doesn't that make the cows sick?"

"No, and it won't make you sick either," I say hastily, knowing how his stomach reacts to suggestion.

"You've probably eaten worse than that in hot dogs," George adds, and we're off on a discourse about junk foods and junk in foods. By contrast, we intone, warming to our theme, the beef we raise contains almost nothing but grass, and you can't get more organic than that. Mike has heard most of it before; he retrieves his smelly strawberry gum from the dashboard and goes on chewing.

My father still calls this the Bender place, after the people who homesteaded it originally, though another man has owned it all my life. This is custom here, and confusing to strangers, especially if such references are used in giving directions, such as, "Go past where the Robinsons used to live, and turn right at the old Smith place. . . ."

After I learned to ride, and as soon as I got my directions straight, I rode here almost every day. The top of the pasture, where the two-track trail runs, is a high plateau with a view of the Badlands to the east. To the north it drops a couple hundred feet into a valley with a dam at one end, a flowing well at the other and a series of natural pools between. A miniature cliff and a natural forest frame the pools with cedar trees, elms, cottonwoods, tumbled rocks and a resident great horned owl. I used to ride with my fishing pole and fish the pools for hours on hot summer days, keeping watch for the owl since he made no sound when he flew. At some point my presence would irritate him, and he would glide silently off, perhaps from right above my head. That was always a good day.

I also used to take off my clothes and wade in the pools or lie on the grass and get a tan. Once Rebel got loose and headed for home; stark naked, I grabbed my boots and raced after her. When I caught her, I rode bareback to where I'd left my clothes and saddle, feeling wonderfully licentious. Then a light plane went over, low. At first I was panicky about being seen naked, even though there couldn't have been much to see, since I was only eleven. Then suddenly I felt free and beautiful; I felt a wild joy from riding naked in the green bowl of the prairie. I may have waved.

I stopped wading and all but gave up fishing the day I saw a churning in what my father had warned me were the twenty-foot depths of a pool. I was sitting on an overhanging rock; bits of dislodged moss floated to the surface as I watched, sunfish skittered away, small turtles fled. Finally, two massive, round, black backs broke the water, two turtles fighting or mating. They were at least three feet in diameter, even allowing for my youthful fear. I watched, edging back farther on my rock, until they sank out of sight again. No one really believed me when I told of it at home. Two years ago my father saw a turtle crossing the dry alfalfa field near the house; he swore it was as big as a washtub. I smiled and said nothing.

The turtles also live at a dike in this pasture.

Fourth Gate

Once while riding here, I noticed on the south face of the dam a number of round white things the size of golf balls: empty turtle shells. Mama Turtle had chosen well; when the babies dug out of their nest they had only to crawl a couple of feet up the bank, across the top—just wide enough for a pickup—and down the north side into the water.

Strictly for the beauty of it, we drive to the edge of the plateau and get out of the pickup. Below us is the dike, and a sinuous trail of water reflecting the dusty green grass as well as the sky. A flicker of movement catches George's eye, and we watch two coyotes taking evasive action. One plunges through a brushy draw and straight up a cutbank, leaving a thin trail of dust in the air. The other, perhaps the female, dives deeper into the gully and flashes in and out of cover as she runs east, away from us.

We don't allow coyotes to be hunted on our land, several of our neighbors discourage it, and still we don't see more than we think are adequate for cleaning up the carrion left from winter and calving. Occasionally someone asks permission to trap, and government employees often stop by to let us know they're shooting coyotes on the leased land in the area, at the request of people who raise sheep and chickens. We try to keep all coyote hunters off our land, and we're vehemently opposed to traps and poison because of the torture and the dangers involved.

I was staying with my uncle George, my mother's brother, when I first learned about coyote poison. I've never forgotten his quiet voice as he told about his conflicts with a government trapper who set traps on the land he leased. He was sitting on the screened-in porch of the log cabin his father had built in a canyon in the southwestern part of the Black Hills. The sun had set and I was sure I could hear bobcats screeching on the ridge across the valley.

"He set some kind of trap up there, and I think he put out some kind of bait. They aren't supposed to. They used to set a cyanide trap, kind of an explosive gun, for coyotes and bobcats. Called them 'coyote getters.' Sheepmen in Wyoming claimed they couldn't get along without them. It's a kind of cylinder with a firing pin underneath that shoots cyanide into the animal's mouth. They put the whole thing inside a piece of meat, and when the coyote pulls up on the meat, the cylinder fires and the cyanide paralyzes the muscles of their throats so they can't breathe."

He packed his pipe and lit it again. "They all said it was a great way to kill coyotes, 'cause with a trap they just chew a foot off and go on their way. I read about a fellow that took one apart while he was hunting, though, so it exploded in his face. I guess it was quite an interesting way to die. Anyway," puff, puff, "it kills coyotes and dogs just fine, because they bite straight down on it. But bobcats bite sideways, and sometimes they'd just gnaw around until they smelled the gun, and leave, and sometimes the gun just fired right out the side of their mouths." Puff.

"I used them for coyotes for a while, when we

had so many, but I quit it about five years ago. I had an old dog I wanted to get rid of, because we were going on a trip and I didn't want to have to have somebody come down and feed him." His voice dropped. "But it was my wife's pet, so I didn't want to shoot it. I was so damn smart. I knew he'd been visiting a dead porcupine down by the creek at night, so I set a coyote getter down there. I thought he'd fire it and die right there, or maybe go up the hill a ways." He shook his head. "Instead he came back here in the middle of the night, and came in through the hole in the screen door I haven't fixed yet and laid down right here on the porch. And he choked and he groaned and howled and carried on out here. I don't know how he ever walked that far. He choked and coughed and knocked stuff over. Finally I had to get up and come out and hit him over the head to finish him off. I had to drag him over the hill and bury him anyway, and my wife wouldn't speak to me for a week." Puff, puff. "That's why I'm against all those poisons. And besides, most of them just keep poisoning everything that eats on whatever you kill in the first place."

We stop to show Mike a badger den—a hole nearly two feet across—hidden in the long grass beside the trail. In my opinion, the badger is the most mysterious of our native animals. I've seen only two in all my time here, yet we find their dens everywhere. Mike would like to see one; I find them terrifying. Cornered, a badger seems to expand his loose skin, then hisses and digs his long, curved claws into the dirt. With his broad head and gray fur, he looks like a miniature grizzly bear that in an instant will stand up and become nine feet tall.

I'd like to give tours of this pasture to people who say cattle ruin the land for wildlife. This pasture could pass for a wildlife sanctuary. Not all land, public or private, is this rich in natural beauty, but I think this pasture is fairly typical of ranchers' use of the land in this area.

By the *American Heritage* definition of "wilderness," this pasture would qualify: "any unsettled, uncultivated region left in its natural condition." Our neighbor turns his cattle into the pasture in late June and removes them in October or November, giving the land plenty of time to recover from grazing. The little streams have more manure in them than deer leave, but they still support an abundance of water life. If this were a public wilderness—or if the public could enter it to enjoy its beauty—the streams would rapidly become clogged with beer cans and toilet paper; the deer, antelope and coyotes would go elsewhere (if there were anywhere left to go); the buffalo grass would be flattened by cars, the cliffs scarred by footpaths, and devastation caused by individuals who enjoy the sound of rolling rocks.

Because this land is privately owned, it remains more nearly wild than most public land. The prairie ecology, which works so well when left alone, functions in a manner close to normal here. It is managed so that the cattle will do no permanent damage; in fact, their manure and their feeding habits encourage plants that might not survive elsewhere. Not every rancher is so careful with his land, or with leased land, but most single-family ranches I've observed in the last forty years are well cared for. What's good for cows is usually good for wildlife, so they can coexist if the number of cows isn't excessive. It's the corporate owners, or the people who buy a place, strip it by overgrazing and then move on, who do the greatest damage. Unfortunately, private ownership also means that not just anyone can enjoy the land. You have to ask permission—but in many cases, if you demonstrate that you will not be careless, permission is not difficult to obtain. Of course, if we let in everyone who promises to be kind to the land, the thundering hordes would trample it to dust. Perhaps some of the hordes who might like to visit will have to be content knowing that someone is taking care of it, that it exists.

Even where predators are concerned, the local people usually wait for actual damages before taking action. I've heard rumors for several years now about a mountain lion sighted a few miles south of here, and two wolves have been reported by neighbors on the east and west. But no one has told the newspapers, and the animals apparently still survive.

Mike is hot and bored, but he doesn't complain. He knows this life is important to us, and my stories somehow fit into it. Gasping with heat as he rides over the silent prairie, he may be thinking of a cool swimming pool filled with friends back in his hometown. But he notices the thick-bodied snake stretched across the two narrow tire tracks of the trail, and hangs out the window as George swerves out of the way to keep from running over it. Mike is torn between desire to kill it and fear that it's a rattlesnake, until we explain that a snake that big, here, is almost invariably a bullsnake, and we wouldn't hurt him if you paid us; he eats his weight in rodents every day. We stop long enough to show Mike four distinct bulges along the snake's length. Last summer he saw a tiny bullsnake as it opened its jaws incredibly wide to swallow a mouse, so he knows what the bulges are.

Crossing this pasture we can look off to the breaks on the south, and down narrow gullies laced with grape, plum and chokecherry bushes on the north. I used to ride up those canyons on my mare after my day's fishing, startling deer and racing beside them until they looked back over their shoulders with big brown eyes and put on a burst of speed. Once, a female antelope approached within five feet of me as I sat motionless on my horse, while the male stamped and whistled upwind about thirty feet. Not until years later, when no one believed my reminiscences, did I realize that racing deer on horseback and being so close to antelope is unusual.

When we get hungry for venison or antelope, we don't hunt here, but perhaps we should—to teach our wildlife more fear. One winter day recently, we found a deer on our land with a hind leg shot off above the ankle. The jagged bone was muddy, and she lay gasping with exertion, eyes dark with fear. Hunting season had been over for two months. We killed and butchered her, so her death wouldn't be wasted.

Now, off to the right of the trail, four big buzzards jump suddenly out of the grass, lurch and wheel off into the sky. They circle, never flapping their wings, turning their heads so yellow beaks show bright against their black bodies. I can feel them examining us, looking for traces of death.

We walk to the spot and identify a dead fawn. The smell makes us gag. It's impossible to say why it died; it's already torn by the buzzards and heaving with smaller predators—the maggots. In a few days only patches of hair will mark the spot.

Mike, to whom death is still a stranger, seems to hold us responsible for the fawn's death. I outline for him the way nature recycles life, remembering the gist of a quote from John McPhee's *Coming into the Country*: ecology means who's eating whom, and when. Here, where nature is allowed to function and dead animals are still left to lie where they drop, the cycle is clear. Sun, wind and rain provide the energy to nourish grass. Deer, as well as insects and small animals, live on the grass and pass its energy on to other animals as they are preyed upon—to foxes, coyotes, owls, snakes. Finally, the fawn's bones and flesh feed the vultures, other scavengers and the soil and grass, which in turn nourish other deer, and the cycle begins again. Everything, when it dies, goes back to grass and earth to feed whatever follows.

"Everything?" Mike asks.

"Everything," I say firmly. "That's why it's a

waste to put people in boxes when they die."

George gives me a look that suggests I should not be more specific. Mike is a little young for the complete lecture on death.

Fifth Gate:
Bones Beneath the
Buffalo Grass

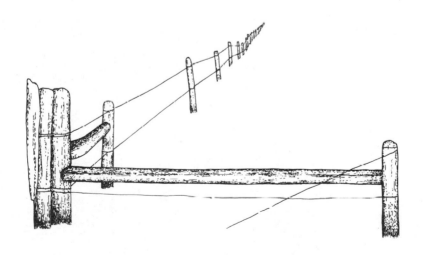

Still on the plateau shimmering with heat waves, and about two and a half miles from the ranch, I help Mike open the gate into my uncle Harold's pasture. To the east and south the country becomes choppy, like a lake in the wind, with eroded mesas and twisting gullies. At the point where the horizon touches the sky, a long straight wall with a pillar at the end shimmers with color: the Badlands Wall. As we watch, several blue chunks of it break off and float away or dissolve. Mike gasps and points; it's his first awareness of mirage. We watch with him as fragments of an entire mythical universe drift away. The wall remains, impervious.

North, across the draw called "the L7," shine the remnants of a site built in the 1960s for Titan missiles, but never armed. The wells at the site, both around four thousand feet deep, have now been purchased by a consortium of area ranchers. By locating here, the missile base forever changed the economy of our small community. The wages paid were so high that ranch hands, sons, fathers—many of the able-bodied men—went to work there while it was under construction. Later, their expectations raised, some of them would no longer accept the wages ranchers could afford to pay, and left the area. Others, reluctant to give up the extra cash, took second jobs in town or urged their wives to do so. Their lives became oriented toward making more money rather than toward building a satisfying life on their land.

The missile base brought other changes too. The paved road leading to it still draws joggers, dog walkers, people who throw off garbage—a recent load included bed springs. The land for the road and site was condemned—simply taken with little compensation—by the government. This damaging legacy is being mitigated now that area ranchers will benefit from the wells that supplied the site. Draglines have been all over the country digging ditches for a pipeline to supply water to members of the users' association. The ugly scars of ditches that will carry the water pipeline to homes and cattle-watering tanks radiate from the missile site in all directions. The earth is scraped and scarred where the ditch was covered over; the area around it is littered with pop cans, boards, human excrement and crumpled magazines contributed to the ecology by the drillers.

We are not members of the association, but the pipeline is our reason for today's trip over east. The ditch was not supposed to cross our land, but somebody misread a map, and an open trench two feet wide and six feet deep across the corner of a pasture has become a trap for our cattle.

A black Angus crossbred calf lies in the barn at home, thin from starvation and dehydration after a few days in the ditch. Only four months old, he is weaned, since he couldn't reach his mother's bag from the ditch. Both shoulders were torn open when he fell; he walks only two or three steps a day, as if they are dislocated. His black eyes don't blink when I shove the bottle of milk replacer in his mouth and massage his throat so he'll swallow. Yesterday he drank a little water and ate a little hay. Perhaps he will live. If he were in good health, he could break my leg with one good kick, and would definitely try it.

My father loaded the calf to bring him home. Alone, he couldn't lift the dead weight, since the calf wouldn't or couldn't help himself, so he did as he has always done: figured out an easier way. He tied one rope around the back legs, one around the body, and another around the front legs, then tied the ends of all three ropes to the pickup. Then, pulling the ropes one by one, he raised the calf as much as he could. He says it took him two hours in the ninety-degree heat to get the calf into the pickup.

This is the latest annoyance. All last summer we made this hot, six-mile trip over east almost daily, because drillers were exploring the area for uranium, and we were afraid they might get lost too. The tracks of their trucks still show in the tawny dry grass, and will probably be there for years. Prairie grass is tough, but fragile enough so that man's damage shows for a long time.

More than the surface scars worry me. The uranium hunters drilled holes as much as four thousand feet deep, searching for bodies of ore. Water tables underlying this area are easily disturbed, lying in porous limestone. Ranchers in other exploration areas talk darkly of aquifers punctured, allowing precious water to drain away or to mix with nonpotable water. This is a dry summer, and several springs that normally water our cattle are dry. But we can't accuse the drillers; we simply don't know enough about what goes on under the surface. No one does.

Going Over East

A young graduate student from the South Dakota School of Mines and Technology began a paper on the possible damages of uranium exploration, with a few thousand dollars donated by a water conservancy subdistrict. The subdistrict wanted to establish a pipeline to the western part of the state from the Missouri River, which flows through the center. We suspected the subdistrict's motives in financing the study, since the drier our area is, the more clamor there will be for such a pipeline. They suspected our interest in the study, since we said adamantly that we do not want to trade our pure, clean water for piped-in Missouri River mud just to mine a little uranium. We hoped the study would demonstrate that exploration would damage the water table and halt the drilling permanently.

The graduate student went quietly about his business, polite and considerate to everyone, and would not say what his findings indicated. Before he could write his final report, he died. He had a history of epileptic seizures, so no autopsy was done. The incomplete report was accepted and the study ended. The test drilling and plans for the pipeline go on.

In the middle of this hot prairie today I'd like to forget politics. Yet it is impossible. I've spent days out here without hearing a motor; now vapor trails crisscross the sky. No one can escape the future or progress, but perhaps we can do a little to shape it. From the air I have seen the tracks of trucks that were driven across the grass only once; even such a simple thing can mark the land for a long time. So each one of us has a responsibility to be sure that the marks we leave on the land are not simple damage, but serve a purpose.

The ancient Greeks believed each citizen's duty—the tax he paid in return for services provided by his government—was to remain informed about and active in the politics of his neighborhood. Of course, the Greeks had women and slaves to take care of the work while they debated current issues, but the principle remains sound: we are our government, and we must be responsible about its policies. In the same way, I believe, we are responsible for the land; if we don't care for it, who will? Ranchers often speak as if they *are* their land, saying things like, "That fire burned seventy-five acres on me," and "Every time that train crosses me it sets me afire." And the land is worthless without water. We regard anything that threatens our water supplies with the same attitude we would have toward a man pointing a gun at our heads.

On the prairie, natural sources of domestic water—for home and livestock use—are few. We have one or two springs, some man-made dams and dugouts filled by rainfall and snowmelt, and a few wells—some of them found by witching. No creeks. No lakes. When a dam goes dry in a pasture that still has grass, we haul three hundred gallons of water to a cattle tank. Every day. But even the wells are precarious. Most aren't deep—a hundred-fifty feet—and water levels have dropped as more people have moved into the country and drilled more wells into the same shallow aquifers.

Water rights generally belong to whomever

settled along a watercourse first, though for irrigation purposes the claimant must prove continuous use, which may be tricky. Grandad may have settled on a stream in 1898 and begun irrigating a garden, but if there was enough water to irrigate in the 1930s, it was a miracle. Though we were told that too few "expert" inspectors were on the payroll to monitor uranium drilling, when it came to water rights, inspectors were sent out to a rancher's land, sometimes without advance notice, to inspect ditches and waterways in an attempt to tell how long irrigation had been going on, and to catch illegal irrigators. With this process, in the last ten years more than 950 water rights in this state have been cancelled, and speculation is rampant that the state has plans for the water once no claims on it exist. Only a few years ago, an unlikely coalition of interests stopped an ambitious scheme to pipe water from the Missouri River in South Dakota to Arkansas, supposedly as a conveyor for coal. Many high-plains ranchers believed adamantly that the coal was only a byproduct, that Arkansas—a region they regard as swampy, unhealthy and peopled by snake-oil salesmen—really wanted the water.

Water battles have only begun. With the entire Great Plains increasing in population and growth of other kinds, water demand is exploding, while much of the law governing water use is unwritten or based on tradition. Also, no one really knows how water moves from one aquifer to another in a specific area, so determining who really owns the water that runs from my faucet is a sticky problem. Most residents of the plains can be smug about water restrictions in other areas, but don't yet realize that we should be conserving water ourselves.

Each small community has a town drunk, and one of our recent ones was the kind who follows a long dry spell with a heavy rain. It would come upon him suddenly; I recall seeing his tractor parked in front of the bar one day during haying season. Once when he'd been to town and gotten thoroughly soaked, he forgot he had the pickup and started to walk home. He got as far as the road that runs past the town water tower, and decided to take a little nap, since it was a warm night. He napped most of the night and the next morning woke up just as his wife, Kitty, walked past on her way to church. Seeing her, he began to groan, "Oh, Kitty, I'm dying. Oh, Kitty, I'm dying of thirst. Please, Kitty, get me a drink of water."

"Cistern's full," Kitty said without breaking stride. "Help yourself."

The cistern is no longer full in the West. About eighty miles from us, just across the state line, is the gas station and cafe that make up the town of Mule Creek Junction, Wyoming. For years we've stopped there whenever we head west, and signs on the tables have always said that water is available only by request. In the washrooms the signs are more direct: We haul every drop of water used here; don't waste it. Across the highway, Wyoming's highway department has built a rest area with composting toilets. Signs inside instruct visitors not to drop cans, bottles or plastic down the holes, and explain that in about three years the waste will be rich soil.

By contrast, when we built our house in South Dakota we studied compost toilets, visited friends who had one, and fully intended to install one. We obeyed the law in getting a building permit from the county, and asked if any special regulations applied to composting toilets. You'd have thought we were speaking Russian. Composting toilets? What's that?

I furnished copies of articles I'd read and a bibliography of literature. Weeks passed; we'd broken ground. I visited the planning office. They'd lost the literature, they thought, and sure, we could put in one of those things, as long as we put in a regular toilet and septic tank and plumbing.

But that's the point; with the graywater tank, wash water is recycled, and with the composting toilet, no water is used.

Sure, as long as you put in a septic tank. . . . We couldn't afford both; we didn't have time to apply to state officials for help, but didn't expect we'd have gotten any, since we've seen no state materials regarding anything more radically energy-conscious than wood stoves and solar panels.

The drive over east seems especially oppressive today. We're in our second summer of unusual drought and unusual heat. The hundreds of spring flowers are gone: low-growing white and lavender phlox; yellow, fragrant sweet peas; purple loco; deep blue cowslips; bluebells; bright yellow western wallflower and clover. Mullein is shooting its gold stalk up from furry, pale green leaves; dandelions and sunflowers droop; pale lavender horsemint and sweet, wild roses are wilting. On a spring day, the odors change every few seconds as you move across the prairie. The trail we're driving was bordered a month ago by tall stems crowded with purple goatsbeard blossoms, beautiful in spite of their name; now the black skeletons rattle in the dry wind that scatters the seeds from the fluffy ball crowning the salsify. The creamy mystery of sego lilies bursts pure and surprising as snow out of the gumbo in June; the waxy white candles of yucca stand six feet tall. Even the yellow prickly pear blooms are gone.

But there's life here: the curled, brown buffalo grass still has a trace of green at its base; wheat grass, hardy little bluestem and blue gramma rustle in the breeze, and big bluestem gives a bronze glow to the hillsides. In some low spots pale bunches of witch grass dance like wild girls with uncombed blond hair. Spikes of thistles stand with pink blossoms drying in the hot wind. The purple petals of snakeroot are drooping around the spiky centers. Silvery oval heads of pussytoes are so nearly hidden in the grass, I'd never noticed them until I read a description by Edward Abbey. Even more secretive, the tiny brown blossoms of clustered broomrape hide near the sagebrush on which they feed.

Knowing the names of the plants that grow here is, for me, a part of learning to understand the prairie in order to care for it intelligently. As if I were studying prairie care I read, and ask the experts. I'm lucky; some of the experts live close by.

My uncle Harold leans back in his chair after Aunt Jo's typical noon meal of home-grown beef and pork, potatoes, green beans and peas from the garden, homemade ice cream with wild plum preserves, and an angel food cake made with eggs gathered that morning.

"You know," he says, "we have to take care of this country or it don't take care of us. If I overgrazed it like them new fellas that moved in down south are, I wouldn't be here in five years. This grass don't come back overnight, you know." He nods at me; sunlight glints off his glasses.

"We keep moving our cows around, taking them off one pasture when it starts getting short, and we don't put them back there until it grows up next spring. Now they have a new theory, that cell theory, says you can put them back in a week. We could run more cows than we do if we chewed off every bit of grass every summer and cut every bit of hay; but then if we had a dry winter and no spring rain, we wouldn't have no grass. If it happened that way a couple of years in a row, we'd have to sell our cows and go to work in town like them new people do." He nods at me, emphasizing. "Pretty soon we'd lose the ranch and somebody would have to come in here and start all over, but with no grass. We're here because we worked at it."

I murmur something, anything to keep him talking.

Fifth Gate

"When those people moved out in the thirties, we were short of money too. But we hung on, and we stayed because we hadn't abused the land. We ate a lot of potatoes! If the country's been good to us, it's because we've been good to it."

Above a limestone cliff, just south of the fence we're driving along, lies a mystery: a little hollow with a trickle of water in good years, several cedars, an elm tree. This niche in the prairie is hidden until you ride into it. On the bottom, no more than fifty feet across, lie the foundations of a cabin, the remains of a tiny dam and two oblongs of piled stone. Each oblong is perhaps seven feet long, three wide, tapering up to two feet high.

Graves? I've shown them to only a few people, half of whom wanted to dig in them and see. My uncle, who's been in this country all his eighty-odd years, knows nothing about them. I've built a fantasy of a couple who had to hide, perhaps from Indians or the law. The canyon niche beyond the little dam is hidden, could have been defended easily by a single person with a gun, and contains water and enough shelter for a horse or two. Perhaps they died here, and someone passed by and buried them, gathering the smooth prairie stones deep over the graves. Perhaps they had a child who buried them.

Or perhaps someone homesteaded here, piled the rocks as a diversion or for use in a house that was never built; perhaps he or she starved out, got bored, went crazy, left.

I'll never know if I have to find out by digging them up.

The prairie is full of stories, though its civilized history is barely a hundred years old. And before that? Still other stories, written on the buffalo grass that breaks under our tires.

Sixth Gate:
Roses Without Thorns

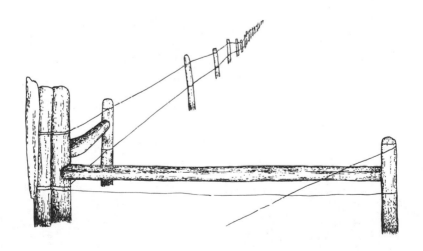

A t the next gate I walk into a cloud of tiny gnats. They are all over me—in my nose, my hair, my ears, tiny pinpricks of pain as they nip at me. I brush my hands across my sweaty face, squashing dozens of them, and open the gate, spitting out their tiny corpses and side-stepping nervously. One day I saw a rattlesnake coiled in the shade of a post here, and have been cautious about that patch of shade for twenty years. Once while fencing, my father found one coiled under an old post he incautiously turned over. He jerked off his shoe and beat it to death with the heel. Later, sheepishly, he admitted that wasn't the best way to kill a rattlesnake.

Rattlesnake stories are common, since the snakes are an almost daily fact of summer living. I tell them too: how I was walking barefoot in the garden, saw a snake in the corn, greeted him cordially and went on picking along his length until I came to his tail and saw the rattles. I grabbed a pitchfork, held him down with it and screamed for help. After killing it, my father pointed out that I could have killed it myself. I must have lost my head because of having naked feet.

I dashed out barefoot to my car one morning and saw a coiled rattler in the path as my foot was descending on him. I somehow precipitated myself upward and to the side. Then I went back to the house, put on my boots, got a shovel, scooped him up—coils, rattle and all—and beat him to death on the concrete apron in front of the garage. I hate to be startled before I've had my coffee. And I've never gone barefoot since.

We don't kill rattlesnakes unless they are right

in the yard, where unwary visitors or my nervous mother might encounter them. In the pastures we leave them alone. We don't kill coyotes, either. Both the snakes and the coyotes serve their purposes here, cleaning up mice and other vermin. We give them the same respect we give responsible humans, and don't bother them if they don't bother us.

Recently I heard a broadcast news story about the development of roses without thorns. The proud researcher expected to make a fortune from his discovery, which he called an "improvement." Besides making several dozen acres of British and American poetry obsolete, he has taken half the essence of the rose away, in my opinion. When we have roses without thorns, prairie without vultures, grass without snakes, spring without skunks, what will be left? Who will care?

Once when I opened this gate, I noticed a night-hawk sitting on a post a few feet up the fence. His head was hunched into his wings, his eyes closed. I shut the gate and walked softly up to him. His body, even in sleep, was streamlined for flight; the long tapering wings were tucked close in, the head elongated, the whiskered beak resting on his breast. I spoke softly to him. He opened one yellow eye, then closed it again. Three hours later, when we came back, he hadn't moved, and we were afraid he was sick. But if he died there, we found no trace, not even a feather, so perhaps he was simply not afraid of us. Maybe he'd heard from the coyotes' howling that we don't kill the animals here.

I've always loved nighthawks. They come out

Sixth Gate

during spring evenings, flying high so their wings are almost invisible strokes of black against the dusk, their location marked by a piercing whistle: *peent, peent.* Then they dive for insects, and pull up with a bug in their beaks and a whooshing boom that can scare the hell out of you as it breaks overhead in the dark.

Riding Rebel home one pitch-black night, I loosened her reins and let her find the way while I relaxed and listened to the night sounds. Far off, I heard coyotes; nearer, insects. The ever-present wind was like the night's breathing around me. And always, from above me or off to one side, echoed the boom of the nighthawks. It was unnerving at first, until my eyes began to distinguish them as darker crescents against the black; then I felt comforted.

A metaphor: we're all blundering in the dark and afraid to trust our horses.

The Indians called them thunderbirds, perhaps because of the booming, or perhaps because they love thunderstorms. Safe inside, I've watched them hover in a thunder- and rainstorm directly outside a window. They face into the hail and wind, and fly just hard enough to remain in place, beating their slender wings against the forces, ignoring the roaring skies. They turn their heads, ruffle their feathers and look as if they were enjoying a shower.

It was years before I found a nest. When I rode across the rocky ridges, the nighthawks would often take off in complete silence. I'd mark the spot with my eyes, dismount and walk carefully to it, but find nothing until the time one flew from under my horse's hoofs. I looked down. The rock was gray with tinges of pale-green lichen; in a low spot lay two gray eggs splotched with darker gray. I maneuvered the horse away, and saw the nighthawk settle gently back as I rode off.

Through the sixth gate we're in the midst of another neighbor's long-legged cattle. In this country some ranchers stick to purebred Herefords, brought in during the 1930s because they were hardy enough to stand summer drought and winter cold, and adaptable enough to grow fat on buffalo grass and muddy water— a quality called "thrifty" by local ranchers. Other ranchers cross Herefords with black Angus for the extra strength; any first-cross animal usually combines the best qualities of both purebred parents. Still other ranchers experiment, regularly changing breeds of bull in an effort to create a bigger, meatier, hardier beef animal.

Styles change. One year the buyers want cattle with "stretch"—rangy creatures with long legs and protruding bones who will presumably collect fat if they're shut in a feed lot with plenty of corn and water. Other years they want a stocky animal, short and weighty.

My father raised purebred Herefords when my mother and I first moved to the ranch; he even had a big sign painted advertising them. But almost before the paint dried, the sign went into the granary and has never emerged. He threw away his syringe, he says, and bought a black bull. (Another of his mottoes, second only to

"Never spend any money," is "Never call a vet if you can do it yourself.") The black bulls helped him by producing hardy calves, small but tough, that jump out of the womb, grab a teat and start growing. Now our cows are a strange varicolored lot, some black with white faces, some all black, a few dark red, and a few with the Hereford lines and coloring.

Of course, occasionally one of the neighbors' bulls gets into our pasture, so we also have a few calves that show strains of Chianina, Longhorn, Limousin and Charolais breeding. Father says, grinning, that this is his way of experimenting without having to buy an expensive bull.

Coming through this gate when we moved the herd to summer pasture in June, I got into some trouble. My husband was gone, to pick up Mike from his mother. I was riding his new horse, Sage, recently purchased and a stranger to me except by reputation. His reputation was none too good, since he'd kicked his previous owner when she walked up behind him, breaking her ribs, damaging her kidney, putting her in the hospital for three weeks. We were reassured that the kick was a fluke; startle any horse on a windy day, and you may be kicked. My father had my horse, Oliver, a gray son of Rebel, tied on behind the pickup in case Sage didn't cooperate.

When we passed through the gate we saw scattered bunches of cattle from the neighbor's herd, and it was my job to get ahead and drive them off before they joined ours. I started out fine, trotting the big horse slowly until I got the feel of him, waving my hand and doing a fine imitation of a Sioux attack, which seemed to awaken some long-buried fear in the cows. They scattered, and I kept behind them, working them along, gathering up bunches and driving them toward a ridge where they'd be out of sight of our cows, moving them slowly so as not to tire them, out of consideration for our neighbor's wallet. Any time a cow runs, she loses weight; in the cow business, weight is money.

I almost had them out of the way when I heard a faint shout and turned. My father was standing on a ridge, pointing, and one of our new, wild, black bulls was making a dead run for the bunch of cattle I was driving. I headed for him, still trotting the big horse. I wasn't sure what he'd do in a run, and he hadn't been on the plains or around cattle much. We rode straight at the black bull. Usually if you do that, a bull will turn and run back toward his own herd. He may make another dodge or two, but once cattle turn they are really on their way; the dodges are just to keep their dignity intact.

Not this wiry little devil. He went around us while Sage was still trying to figure out what to do with his feet, and went straight on. He was heading for a big Chianina bull in the center of the neighbor's herd, and wanted a fight. His nose was level with his back and he was bellowing and snorting. We'd trot up beside him, and he'd sidestep and be gone.

I trotted the horse faster; the bull increased his speed. Finally I walloped the horse with the reins and we were on the bull at once. The dance began.

It's beautiful to watch a good cutting horse in the arena, anticipating the cow's moves, turning her back in a way that looks rehearsed. But it's not fun on a horse you've barely met, especially when it involves a bull blowing snot and bellowing at every jump. I wanted my agile little gray horse; I knew him and trusted him. But I didn't have time to get him. Sage and I lost ground until we were almost to the neighbor's big bull. Our little black bull wanted him bad.

Suddenly Sage seemed to take hold, to grasp what I was trying to do. It felt as if he had sprouted claws that dug into the ground. He slashed in front of the black bull like a great scythe, whipped around the other side and slid to a stop, then back the other way, faster than the bull could turn. His legs seemed to be parallel to the ground, and I was so sure he was going down I could already hear my leg snap.

But he kept it up, again and again, while I hung on and shouted encouragement. Now that I think back on it, the encouragement consisted of "Get that black bastard, you son of a bitch!" or words to that effect. My father, who never allowed hired men to swear in front of me, later remarked on how sound carries on the prairie.

Suddenly the bull had had enough. He whipped around and headed back to our cows, tired, wanting to take it easy. But the horse was one demon ridden by another; we were right behind that bull every jump until he staggered into line with the herd.

Unfortunately, like many thrilling stories, this

one had a bad ending. Sage proved virtually worthless as a cow horse. Once he'd been turned into a pasture it took two of us three hours to catch him, and he always tried to strike at us with his front feet while being bridled. If this were a western romance, I could lie and say we worked patiently with him, day after day, until he forgot his bad habits and became a wonderful horse. We're patient, but we don't have that kind of time to waste, nor do we care to take unnecessary chances. We sold him to a good home.

It's easy to romanticize and distort the West; our history invites it, being filled with gunmen, cattle rustlers, conflicts over land, bawdy houses and madams with hearts of gold. People who visit the West briefly and then write about it tend to do so in sweeping generalities: purple mountains have majesty above fruited plains, good-hearted if occasionally profane people ride noble horses into the sunset. The longer I live here, the more I fear such generalities, and study details in my lifelong attempt to understand my surroundings more completely.

When someone from New York sits in my living room, looks out the windows and speaks in broad generalities about isolation, my brain whirls. I do know about physical isolation; the phone and electric lines go down in blizzards, leaving us without piped-in power or the opportunity to share our fears with someone miles away. But our house is filled with books by brilliant thinkers, and the fact that my husband and I are together most of our workday has forced us to discover an intimacy—not always without friction—that most couples can't achieve. These things keep real isolation at bay most of the time.

Broad generalities and shallow theories confuse and anger me. Reality hinges on practicality, on knowledge that has daily use. Many people here dehorn and castrate calves just before or after the new moon to cut down on bleeding, butcher during the first three days after the full moon for tender meat, harvest and kill weeds when the moon is old, in its third or fourth quarter. This is reality, the real West—sturdily defying the shallow theories dreamed up by metropolitan thinkers in high-rises, people whose well-shod feet and clean hands never touch earth or blood.

Seventh Gate:
Of Cows and Singing
Clouds

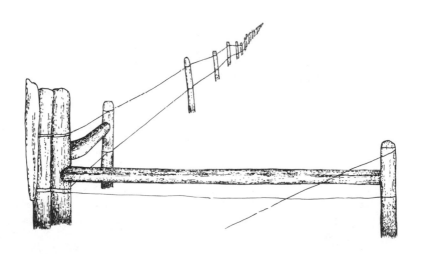

At the seventh gate, Mike is startled by a jack rabbit that waits until he has taken the gate chain off to leave its shady spot under the brace posts in a series of twenty-foot leaps. Mike wants to chase it, but it has a head start and can travel forty-five miles an hour. The rabbit's gray now, but in winter I'm always surprised to see them half hidden, white except for the pink flesh of their ears, outlined by a tracery of gray fur.

Once through this gate, about four and a half miles from home, we're in a five-thousand-acre pasture, looking south toward the Cheyenne River in the blue distance and the green groves around the home of the manager of this "big outfit," a corporation ranch.

Nearer still is the old homestead of one of the Scandinavian families who came west with my grandfather—seven weeks on horseback trailing their cattle—looking for homesteads. The parents and seven children all filed claims in the wide grassy valley which now makes up the big pasture. Homestead law required homesteaders to cultivate their acreage, put up a house and live on the land five years. Some folks, then as now, interpreted the law loosely. Stories abound of land cultivated by turning over a couple of spadefuls of dirt. Neighboring homesteaders often shared a sod house on the line between two claims, and took turns working in a nearby town.

But this family came to stay. They put up a house and barn, and every year when they cleaned the corrals, they hauled the manure out to a hillside and dumped it in the shape of their brand, a hat: ⌒ .

The corrals are gone, and the house. Only the shell of the barn remains. And the brand—still visible eighty years later, outlined in the greenest grass. The irony of the family making its mark in cow manure strikes me each time I see the brand; manure was probably the only thing they had in excess.

The family's graves are nine or ten miles across country in the Hermosa cemetery, on a little hill above the town. I've often wandered there, thinking of the stories that lie under the big granite stones, if one could listen hard enough. My father speaks of his Memorial Day visits to the cemetery as "visits to my future." Or he'll gesture to a series of headstones and say, "There they all are. They used to be important in the county; they used to be rich."

I wonder about his thoughts as he looks at the tombstones of people with whom he worked and rode and laughed. I used to feel frustration when he wouldn't tell me the details of some stories; all that good material was going to waste! How could it matter to anyone if I wrote their stories, once they were dead? But now I feel a kinship with them. Their stories were their lives. Why should I entertain anyone, even myself, with fictionalizing them, dressing them in thoughts and attitudes they might not have had?

Telling Mike about the brand sculpted on the hillside by loads of manure has started me thinking about a topic that doesn't get much public attention. The average person's closest contact with human or animal waste is pushing down on a handle that draws clean water to wash it away. Or you get a little on your shoe and scrape it off on the grass, cursing the neighbor's dog. This distance from even our own wastes has become so commonplace that we have developed a real distaste for the entire subject; it has become one of our worst profanities, and the basis for insults directed specifically against rural people. One of my favorite guides to human thought and sources of inspiration, Bartlett's *Familiar Quotations*, has only one reference to it, an indirect one at that. Perhaps the difference between people who live on the land and people who don't can be summed up by their attitude toward this byproduct of life.

I'm not exactly fond of manure, even when I'm smiling as I shovel it on the garden. But by being around cattle, I have learned to live with it. I remember when I gave away my favorite pair of open-toed summer shoes. Every time I wore them, I had to get out to open a gate on the way to town, and discovered when my toes began to squish that a cow had been there before me. Manure, in various forms, is an inescapable part of ranch life.

Spring storms soak the dirt-dung mixture in our corrals until it is viscous two feet down. Even wading carefully through this muck in four-buckle overshoes moves some of it to pant legs and inside boots. When we grab a calf to give it a pill, we murmur prayers that we won't fall down. When I've got my face plastered against a cow's flank, trying to get her calf to suck, and I hear the familiar *plop! plop!* I wrinkle my nose, as anyone would. But the smell of a corral means spring and a richer garden, and the only time I'm made aware of our casual attitude is when I glance down at my feet in town and realize I'm advertising my job. I suspect that many folks who love Nature (with a capital N) aren't thinking of manure, any more than they're considering teeth and blood and death, but it is another part of life we should not leave out of our calculations for the future. We have been privileged to ignore waste of all kinds in this country, to be able to use pure water to wash away the sight and smell of something that is hoarded and turned to good use in other countries. Can we go on this way?

People who occasionally ride over east with us wonder, after miles of driving through pastures without a cow in sight, why it's necessary to shut every one of these gates. Partly it's habit; we don't always know who has cattle where, so we shut gates without thinking about it. That's misleading, though, because often we do know. It's our business to know where cattle are, so we know what problems to expect moving through a neighbor's land.

But you'd think sometimes, when it's 110 degrees, we'd risk leaving a gate open. On hot days a cow is unlikely to wander far from water between 10:00 A.M. and dusk. The problem with that theory is that cows seem to have an instinct for open gates. Leave a gate open without a cow in sight for five miles, and you'll drive back to the gate five minutes later to find twenty-five cows trotting out. It is, of course, ridiculous to think they crouch in gullies waiting until you go past, then spring up and race for the gate. On the other hand, how do they get there so fast?

Many times when we've been working cattle through a gate, cutting some one way and some another, we've also noticed a cow's ability for speed. A cow will head for the gate, shambling slowly. You don't want her to go through it, so you stroll in that direction. She trots. You trot. She seems to roll her eyes at you, and at the precise instant you haven't got a chance of catching her, she gallops through the gate. She has it timed to the second and knows just how fast you can go, and how short of wind you are.

Once in a while a cow will make a mistake. I landed on my knees eyeball to eyeball with a horned cow once. She plowed mud, stopping to avoid me, and neither of us breathed for a minute. Then she snorted snot all over me and ran off, bellowing.

As we drive, we're accompanied by the invisible birds, a rare species here. I began calling them that because, even on horseback, I could hear their cheerful twittering but could never see them. I'd look up; the sky would be vacant, but skeins of song seemed to swoop around and hang over me. Actually, I suppose the little gray birds hide in the grass and call back and forth. Only in summer and early fall are they noticeable. Before that, the blackbirds and meadowlarks dominate sound on the prairie.

The red-winged blackbirds, with an occasional gold head among them, are the first back. One morning in March, with snow still on the ground and winter weighing on me like my soggy wool coveralls and my mud-covered, five-pound boots, I step outside and hear incredible music. I look around and find blackbirds perched in one bare tree, hundreds of them, calling, whistling, singing, hooting obscenely. They are always together at first, rising in a singing cloud out of one tree and into another. Then they separate, mate, scatter out into the fields to hang their cupped nests from growing grass or alfalfa.

The minute the first blackbird arrives, I declare spring officially open. I can sing through the blizzards that invariably follow, whistle while I dig a truck out of a snowbank, smile while I wallow in blood helping a cow calve. I exchange raucous and off-color remarks with the blackbirds while dragging myself through knee-deep corral mud. Later on, the meadowlarks take over, trilling and flashing their yellow breasts from every post. When they come they seem to be everywhere, along with the killdeer crying by the dams and the curlews wheeling overhead, the sparrows, sparrow hawks, red-tailed hawks and the whole varied bird tribe. But my uncle says he knows more birds came with spring in his youth, "before all that bug spray, and before everybody thought they had to save every blade of alfalfa by spraying for grasshoppers."

Except for the blackbirds, calving season can be pretty grim, but I always chuckle over the saying, "You are what you eat." Most people tend to apply the slogan selectively; our friends are glad to come for supper, but even the beef eaters don't want to know what we named the cow on their plate. Our vegetarian friends (Mike calls them "vegetations") sometimes eat our organic beef. As long as they don't lecture me on my eating habits, I avoid commentary on theirs and cook two vegetable dishes for dinner. On the prairie, everything eats something else, but the meat-eating predators—including humans—are at the top of the food chain. While we always have several offers to help with branding, few people offer to help us butcher.

Steers are always worth more at the sale ring than heifers, so we butcher only heifers. (There's a militant feminist metaphor in there somewhere.) I often remember something specific about each heifer we eat at our first meal of her. We may have pulled the calf from the mother to save her life. We probably shook her until the birth fluid ran from her lungs and she took her first gasping breath, rubbed her down with an old gunny sack to get her warm and dry. A few days later, if the cow wasn't letting the calf suck, I may have knelt in the manure-laced straw and slashed my fingers on the calf's teeth while stuffing a teat into its mouth. We branded the calf, ear-marked it, vaccinated it against disease and turned it out in the pasture to watch it grow.

As the heifer grew up, she may have demonstrated enough personality to acquire a name. We have Can Opener, with a single sharp horn; Zebra had an oddly colored coat that looked striped from a distance; Amazing Grace is the gentle daughter of Sweetheart, who is the daughter of Ugly, who, after almost ten years of jumping fences and tearing down gates, has gone to her just reward—the sale ring. Most cows are named for their attributes or temperament, or because they resemble a relative or prominent person. Dolly Parton was not named for the reason that may spring to vulgar minds, but because her front legs were spangled with spots, like fancy western pants. Naming cows isn't too unusual, even among tough old ranchers. One friend used to name his bulls after the person who accompanied him to the sale ring when he bought the bull. The year I went with him, he reluctantly decided it would be too embarrassing to stand in the pasture calling a bull named "Linda," and settled on "Hazel," which seemed to him more masculine. Sometimes the name is merely a descriptive phrase, including "that old brockle-faced bitch," or "that damned cow with the short horns." Another nearby family faces facts from the beginning; calves raised for meat are always named for their destiny: Steak, Hamburger, Stew Meat.

In other words, we participate in the animal's life, from conception through maturity and death. We are responsible for its life in the fullest sense. We acknowledge our responsibility for its death. We feel we have the right to eat a cow that would not have lived at all without our help. We do so with respect, as well as with enjoyment.

Eighth Gate:
Homesteading the
Future

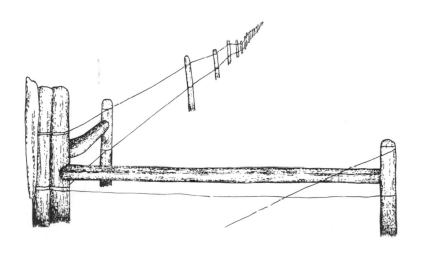

*T*he pickup sounds as if it's boiling, and the prairie shimmers with heat waves. Mike gets another drink while I open the gate, and we're in our pasture again, five and a half miles from home.

But we don't own this land; it's a school section, set aside for the support and establishment of schools in the homesteading era. Even in this vast wilderness, most schools are now consolidated, with students bused miles from their rural homes to the city. The school sections are leased to ranchers to increase the state's tax revenues. This is a convenient arrangement for many ranchers, a way of increasing their grass and the number of cattle they can run without the burden of a mortgage on the land, high interest rates on a loan or increased taxes. However, school leases are a two-edged sword. The state retains mineral rights and can lease them to anyone without permission from the rancher who is paying to graze the land.

It did not surprise us, then, when we found a uranium exploration drill rig set up in our pasture last summer. We were polite: did they realize they had no right to be there? They were brisk: they had every right, since they had leased the mineral rights. They turned away, too busy to talk to an ignorant rancher and a woman about these complex matters.

My father persisted, politely. Across the fence—he pointed—was the school section. The land they were on was ours, complete with mineral rights, and we haven't leased them to anyone. Maps were unrolled and spread on a pickup hood, and within a few minutes they were packing up.

My father's smile sometimes makes people think he is a gentle man, and he is, to women and children and animals and most men. But a few years ago a major company put a propane line across pastures near the highway next to our ranch. When the men seeking permission to cross private land dealt with my father, they tried to pressure him; they were pushy. He visited his lawyer. Today the propane line runs for miles across private land, but when it reaches our fence line, it jogs into the highway right-of-way.

Another drawback of using school sections is that any potential buyer may at any time petition that the land be sold at auction; the man who has been using it must then purchase it, or lose it. One of my mother's brothers lived an example. He pastured a particularly fine canyon in the southern Black Hills for years, until someone decided it would make a good subdivision. Individuals could pay more for a one- to ten-acre piece of it than he could afford to pay per acre for the entire 640 acres. The people who have moved in probably think he is a greedy land baron, who would have deprived them of homes in the country for a few cows and the pleasure of riding his range in lonely splendor. Daily, as he drives past trailers and small homes, three-wheelers and dogs, he must envision the valley as it once was: unfenced, untracked except by cattle and wild animals. The mountain lion family that lived on the ridge above the valley hasn't been seen for a while.

Buying a little piece of land in the country

seems to be everyone's dream. After the house is built, it's natural to want a horse, maybe a milk cow or chickens and a big dog to protect an isolated paradise. Since it's the country, they think it's kind to let Rover run free. Rover runs a few deer to death, meets some amiable companions and begins running calves to death, or killing them outright. He is soon shot or poisoned by a rancher, or perhaps dognapped. This sort of thing makes for hard feelings between old and new country dwellers.

Besides wanting dogs, some of the new people want better gravel or paved roads, and want the county to plow them in winter so their children can go to school, or so they can get to their jobs in town. Longtime county residents who have been digging out their own roads for years to get their own children to school find this trend disturbing. More county maintenance and better roads require higher taxes, and the folks who live in a trailer on an acre of land pay a lower percentage of those costs than ranchers.

The new residents may demand buses to get the kids to school. Used to garbage pickup in town, they expect it in the country. Some, pressed for time, dispose of their garbage by tossing it down a gully, to be found by the delighted Rover and his buddies and spread across the countryside. Or washed onto someone else's land.

So our minds are troubled when we drive across these "empty" school sections. I think many of these problems are related to mutual accountability, or the lack of it. Many of us simply aren't aware of the size and scope of our responsibilities to one another.

For example, if we own and operate a car, we are responsible for not only whether it runs over someone, or is driven drunk, but for keeping its fuel emissions low, its oil level high enough to protect the engine, its tires fixed. If we don't know how to do these things, we should learn, at least enough so we are not entirely dependent on someone else to take care of us. Say the earth is a car. Lots of us know how to drive, but most of us have no idea how to change a tire, check the oil or add water to the radiator.

For ranchers and others involved with the soil, responsibility is often directly related to good sense or the lack of it. For example, if we overgraze a pasture this dry year, we run the risk of getting insufficient moisture to bring the grass back in the spring. If we have no spring grass, we may have to sell cattle before we're ready, losing money. If we throw tin cans and other garbage out the pickup window as we're driving through a pasture, we may lose a cow who eats a can or gets one stuck on her foot and gets a crippling infection. So we can't imagine throwing garbage out the window onto someone else's land or along the highway.

I'm curious about the relationship between the roadside garbage that seems to constantly increase everywhere, and our concepts of land ownership. Native Americans confused and annoyed white negotiators by refusing to accept the concept of land ownership. A few of them, under the influence of large quantities of liquor, finally grasped the idea clearly enough to sign their names to pieces of paper that have been causing trouble ever since. As soon as the whites got everything organized properly, land was divided into neat mile-square sections, and every square inch of it was assigned either to an individual or to public ownership. Most adults immediately began working hard so they could eventually own at least enough land for a house.

Meanwhile, we seem to have lost any sense that we are responsible for the land around us, even if we do not own it, and especially if it is public land. Rather than caring for all land as though it were ours, large numbers of us now seem to regard public land as a place where you go to do what you would not or could not do on your own.

Now we're passing the tiny secret gully where water drips through a hill into a limestone basin, and grouse hide to nibble buffaloberries. One year, when the grouse were numerous, we shot six and made a sauce of the berries they'd eaten, still undigested in their crops. They were delicious, but we've never felt right about hunting them since. Their numbers are too few, and they've grown almost tame. In winter they come into the yard, picking around the haystacks and being snowed under. Some mornings we find small craters where they've exploded upward from a drift as if their tails were on fire. When people ask us if they can hunt grouse on our ranch, we say, "Gosh, we haven't seen a grouse for years!" We also know where fox kits tumble around the entrance to a den on spring evenings, a secret even from our chicken-raising relatives.

North of us is a small pasture we use sparingly, partly because its only water source is a small dam that's dry most of the year. When we first bring cattle over east in spring, we often put the two-year-old heifers in here briefly, because it's the only pasture we have that's almost completely surrounded by our own land. By putting the heifers here, we may be able to keep the neighbors' bulls from getting in. We want to keep the heifers open—not pregnant—until we're ready to turn our own black bulls in, to provide the heifers with small-boned, easily birthed calves. When the dam gets low, we turn the heifers out and put a horse in this pasture until there's no more water for her to sip from the dam.

Despite its small size, 120 acres, this is a spectacular pasture. It contains part of a long ridge that begins at the third gate we came through this morning, nearly four miles west of here; we've been driving along its flat top for nearly an hour. The ridge drops off to the valley below—another rancher lives in the valley—and is wrinkled with tiny canyons and limestone outcrops that shelter deer, grouse, porcupines, buffaloberries, plums, grapevines. Only once in thirty-odd years have we found a calf with his nose packed with porcupine quills. His entire head was swollen, his tongue hanging out and filled with quills, and he was unable to eat or drink. We loaded him in the pickup with little trouble, and took him home to the chute, which would immobilize him. Once he was shut in, we took turns yanking quills out for two hours. He bellowed and snorted at the first few, then calmed down and bore it stoically. We told ourselves he knew we were helping, but he was probably already numb to the pain.

Just north of the ridge is a steep-sided, perfectly conical hill that seems to appeal to golden eagles; we've seen them perched there often over the years. The hill offers no concealment for their enemies, and an excellent predator's view of the countryside. We never get full use of the little pasture—that is, our cattle never eat all the grass before the dam goes dry. We might use the pasture more efficiently if we drilled a well. But aside from the expense, the pasture provides feed and serves as an uncrowded buffer for wildlife, and if we can't afford that we probably can't afford to ranch at all.

One of the little side canyons on the ridge's rim evidently served as a homesteader's garbage dump. All the goods that became trash arrived there at the end of a two-day, twenty-five-mile horse and buggy trip from Rapid City, the nearest large town. I've spent happy hours there, picking up pieces of old stoves, blue glass jars and tiny bottles. They've been jumpy hours, though; such a dump is a perfect place for rattlesnakes. In fact, many of our rattlesnake encounters have been over east. Once when my father and I had brought cattle over with the horses and were riding back, we encountered one on the flat top of the ridge. We were galloping—he on his big half-Tennessee Walker, Zarro, and I on little Rebel, trying to keep up—when we saw the snake coiled in the road between them. Both horses reared up in the air and spun around. When we all settled down, Father and I started looking for rocks. Not a rock in sight. I think we finally picked up a post lying by the fence and beat the snake to death with that, and then felt guilty about it. I've never killed a snake in the pasture since.

I've ridden past bigger rattlers on long slopes with plenty of rocks, but simply wished them a good day. It seems unnecessary to kill a snake that's minding its own business—catching mice, obvious from the three or four bulges along its length.

As far as we know, we've never had a cow snakebit, but my sorrel gelding was bitten on the nose once. He was pastured near the house, and one morning I saw two tiny cuts just above his upper lip. His nose swelled to the size of a basketball for a couple of weeks, then gradually went down, and he suffered no other obvious ill effects.

That was a hard-luck horse; his bones lie just north of here in the next pasture. He was a wild colt, since he was out of the wild red mare, Rebel's dam; naturally, I named him Yankee. The mare ran him into a wire, and the vet said it would probably damage his gait. But I loved him and kept him. I even showed him in colt classes at the county fair. Once, midway through the class, I was standing with my back to him, and suddenly I noticed people pointing and gasping. When I turned, Yankee was on his hind legs, pawing at me with his front feet. My father never trusted him and wouldn't let me break him to ride. Instead, he was sent to an old horse-breaker in the Badlands, and even when he came back he was not the gentle, loving horse Rebel was. I did ride him, but he never believed I could be trusted.

Eighth Gate

Yankee's career was colorful. Once a hunter passing through the ranch without our permission left a gate open, and the two horses wandered out toward the highway. Rebel came back, but Yankee didn't. I found him several days later, standing alongside the railroad tracks, terribly cut and bruised as if he'd been hit by a train. I led him home and doctored his wounds for months. Eventually, we brought him over east for our summer horse, and during a thunderstorm—on my birthday—he was struck by lightning and killed. His skull now hangs in my study, along with my collection of skulls, pelvic bones and feathers. Mother Nature has a tendency to demand that we become philosophical about these things.

My shirt is stuck to me with sweat; George mops his forehead; Mike is restless, squirming on the seat. I point south, until Mike can see the lookout rocks.

He wants the story, but there isn't one. The pile of rock has been there as long as Harold, my eighty-year-old uncle, can remember. It stands three feet high at the point of this long ridge, and is visible for several miles. We climbed up to it once; it's built of naturally flattened chunks of limestone, carefully leveled and chinked with smaller rocks, and tapers up to a point at the top. Harold says sheepherders used to build landmarks like it, but no sheep have ever been herded in this neighborhood. It's impossible for us to tell its age, unless something was put inside it, but we won't tear it down for that. I've long feared some hunter would shoot at it, as the whites shot at Chimney Rock when they crossed the Nebraska plains—not for any good reason, just to see if they could hit it.

It's a mystery, like the grave-size piles of rock behind us. I'm content not knowing, and surprised to be. Can it mean I'm becoming mature, when I don't need to know all the answers?

Ninth Gate:
Never Count the Dead
Ones

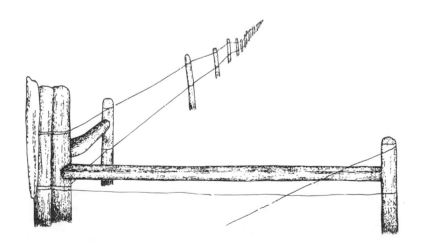

Now we open another gate—it's so tight. George has to help me—and we're in what we call the Lester place, where I had my first experience driving cattle in a blinding snowstorm. The Lester story has unfolded over the years as we've driven cattle here, fenced, worked on improving the water system.

Silas Lester came into this country in the second and last homesteading period, the 1920s. He plowed the bottom land and planted a kind of alfalfa that is strange to us today and that none of us can precisely name; it is tall and hardy, and it's still here after sixty years without care. Silas dug out springs by hand, put in wooden pipe and irrigated some of the meadows. He put up a frame house and corrals, and began building a stone house. Three half-completed walls still stand, the native limestone cut into neat square blocks and laid up in straight rows. He must have had experience. A door is evident, but the walls didn't get high enough for us to tell if he planned windows. I imagine he did, though, because his valley is beautiful.

At some point he obtained a mail-order bride. It was customary at the time for lonely women to place advertisements in papers circulated in the far West. Lonely men answered; eventually some sort of agreement was reached, of love-by-mail or convenience. The prospective bridegroom often sent a railroad ticket. There are stories of women who cashed in dozens of such tickets and went on living happily right where they were.

Others came west. I can only imagine the trip:

the long slow train chugging across green but flat eastern Dakota, crossing the river into the dry brown prairie, with the promise of cool blue mountains in the distance. There your heart might lift—trees! The country might look like home after all. Then, before you reached the mountains, you would get off at the bleak little Hermosa station. The Black Hills were visible in the west, but east and south lay nothing but dun-colored prairie, mostly treeless.

Silas probably met the train with his wagon, a tall, stooped man, bony, with big capable hands. And what did he see? Chances are, Maude was a big woman when she arrived, but the story goes that before long she weighed more than three hundred pounds, so life in this valley must have had some good points. When Silas drove the buggy to town, he sat on the seat and Maude took up most of the back.

They had a daughter, planted a big garden, worked hard. Like many homesteaders, they may have mortgaged their place to buy seeds or equipment. The dry years of the 1930s, one after the other, with dust covering the fences like snowdrifts, must have become too much to bear. They sold out to the Hasselstroms for two dollars an acre and left. Their story is repeated in dozens of remains from the homesteading years scattered around the ranches in this area: a sunken spot that may have been a root cellar, a few old posts where stout corrals stood, the rusting fragments of a Model A Ford, the stone of an unfinished house slipping back into the earth.

Standing beside the shell of the stone house, we look at what the Lesters saw. To the east runs a long, shallow valley; the Badlands glow with vague pastel colors in the distance. Around them lay their tiny homestead, lovely but less than a mile wide. On three sides they couldn't see out of it; the low prairie hills shut out everything but sky. Their only change may have been a rare trip to town in the horse-drawn buggy and, later, the car.

George listens with patience to my stories; Mike is clearly bored. "Think about it," I insist. "Even in the winter we can get out, go to town, watch television, call someone. They couldn't even see the Black Hills. You know, don't you, that they had no telephones then? No TV. If they wanted to see someone, they walked maybe five miles there and back."

Mike knows, but doesn't understand, though last winter when he came to visit us, he had to walk to the house from the highway because our road was drifted in. Now, he has found several pieces of strawberry gum in his pocket and stuffed them all in his mouth. I tense as he blows a bubble, which promptly explodes all over his dirt-streaked face.

Then I make myself relax. I was always drinking water when I was Mike's age and came with my father on these trips; no doubt that annoyed him. I seldom chewed gum because of maternal concern over the state of my teeth, and never bubble gum because of maternal concern over the state of her own nerves. Now I understand. But Mike hasn't been reared as strictly as I was, and I can't change his habits in a summer. Perhaps someday he will remember bits of my history and ecology lessons and make some use of them in his world.

The trees Silas planted are now huge old cottonwoods, seven of them scattered through the valley. One has planks nailed across an opening in the trunk where a calf, scratching, got his head caught and remained for days. We got him out alive, but he staggered to the dugout to drink, and died there. One old tree died last year, and we feel its loss like that of an old friend. The others are probably soon to follow. We should find time, in a wet year, to plant more in the bottoms of the gullies, where they might survive without much care. They would have to be fenced, since the cattle would otherwise chew or rub them down.

We check the dugout my father found by witching for water. It's the lowest I've ever seen it, but who knows if the drought or uranium exploration is to blame? We found a cow in the dugout on a day like this— a hundred degrees in the shade and there ain't no shade, as the cowboys say. She was in the water, her back legs spread out behind her. We figured she'd slipped on the steep side of the dugout and was simply stuck in the mud. We went to work to get her out, a nightmare.

She was a wild black cow. When we backed the pickup as close as we dared and went down to try to get a rope around her, she swung her head and bellowed, spraying us with mud and froth, then thrashed the water with her front legs.

We backed up, considering. We needed to get

the rope around her belly, or her neck and one front leg; if we roped just her head we might strangle her before we got her out. But that was the easiest and safest thing to do, so we tried it anyway. Father roped her and hitched the rope to the pickup. I watched her while he put the truck in gear. She bellowed, choked, struggled. The pickup motor whined, the tires spun. Nothing else happened. He turned off the motor and went to stand in the sun looking down at her.

"I ought to shoot her," he said. "I'll probably kill her getting her out of there, or she'll kill me, or she'll die anyway. But I don't have a gun. And beating her to death wouldn't be very merciful." He grinned wryly.

"If you dropped the rope down the steep side, maybe I could wade out there and get it under her belly," I suggested timidly.

"No. Too much chance of you getting hurt."

While we were trying to throw old fence posts under her to give her purchase to get out, a neighbor came by on horseback. He was a husky, fearless type. He took the rope without asking us and did a wild dance in the mud with the cow. Somehow he got out alive, and the cow had a rope around her belly. Eventually, with the pickup in super low, we got her out, dragged her to dry ground well away from the dugout, and carefully removed the rope. She lay spraddled out on the ground, bellowing and shaking her head, her back legs at right angles to her spine.

After a pause for consideration and conversation, my father and the neighbor approached her, grabbed her tail and tried to tail her up.

"Back's broke," observed the neighbor, stuffing a fresh quid of tobacco into his cheek and peeling mud out of his hair and teeth.

"Probably," said my dad, but he wasn't quite ready to give up.

We came back every day for a week, bringing her hay and buckets of water. She ate and drank, and dug the ground around her front feet into a dusty bowl, but her back legs never changed position. Her calf stood beside her, bawling piteously and trying to tip her up far enough to get a teat, until he weaned himself and wandered off.

Finally my father shot her and dragged her off behind a hill so she wouldn't wash back into the dugout in the spring rains. I lamented the loss of a valuable young cow and the money we'd lose on her calf, who would be hungry the rest of the summer and thinner than the others in the fall. But my father pronounced another of his rules for ranch living: "Never count the dead ones."

The only other water in this pasture, since a natural spring dried up recently, trickles out of a pipe placed by Silas Lester into a metal tank we installed when the wooden one he'd built began to rot. One day when we were having trouble thawing the pipe—it was thirty below zero with a strong north wind—we noticed an owl sitting on the hillside ten feet away, above the tank. We worked there for over an hour, making frequent trips to the pickup to warm up or get tools. He only turned his yellow eyes to watch; he didn't fly off. We finally noticed a mole caught under one of his claws. When we drove away, presumably he finished his breakfast. We've often seen great horned owls in the trees; they glide silently off their nests if we get too near. It delights me to know we are not driving them away, and convinces me that the use we are making of this land is not disturbing its original native inhabitants.

A few years ago a pair of great horned owls nested on our land near Hermosa. It was always a pleasure to hay there in summer and watch them drift out of the trees to drop on a mouse. Then one day, on the highway bridge just outside of town, I saw a bundle of feathers that looked familiar. I stopped and ran back; it was a great horned owl, shot through one wing. He had fluttered that far, then probably had been hit by a car. I found the other hung contemptuously by his wings on our barbed wire fence, and the remains of a bald eagle scattered in the grass.

On days like today we drive to the tank whether we need to check it or not, to drink the cold, pure water in our cupped hands or the long-handled dipper fastened to the post. Mike isn't convinced that water running out of a pipe in a pasture can be safe to drink, and he watches us skeptically. When we've quieted our thirst, he takes a few sips, ducks his head underwater then comes up sputtering and shakes like a puppy. While we sit on a rock resting, he goes off to study some tracks in the mud, then drags George over to identify them: coyote, skunk, porcupine. The wild animals prefer to drink the water that runs over the edges of the tank rather than what's in the muddy dugout.

Despite the scarcity of water, people have always planted trees in this country. To look at the homestead sites now, bare except for a sunken cellar, a few stones arranged in a rough square for a foundation, one might think those pioneers preferred their wide open spaces without trees. Other things came first, of course: first a house, then the required cultivation, then a barn or shed for the animals, a root cellar for food storage, perhaps corrals, certainly fences. The daily work kept them busy. But almost without exception, stories about pioneering by the early settlers themselves mention flower seeds ordered through the mail, or saved from the rare apple, planted and watered with care. They tried, but in a dry year, if they were hauling water some distance even for use in the home, it simply might not have been possible to save a tree, even by dumping the wash water on it, as many women did.

When the homesteaders moved away, the trees might not have survived if their roots had not reached underground water. The roots of an old cottonwood tree seventy feet tall might reach twenty or thirty feet into the ground. Cut down a big tree that has stood beside a creek, and as you saw it up, water literally runs from it. Only with such extraordinary self-watering power could these trees have survived long periods of drought like the 1930s, and only certain trees—cottonwoods, cedar, pine—have survived without being planted and tended by humans.

Ninth Gate

The other side of the trees' ability to survive is another matter. Often I hear environmentalists make statements like, "If we have our way, no one will ever cut another tree in the Black Hills." This is not a popular statement with loggers and other folks who make a living from lumbering, but it also has wider implications. In the Black Hills to the west of our ranch, the policies of federal and state park officials in the past have centered on saving trees by putting out forest fires and prohibiting cutting. Lately, water enthusiasts such as fishermen, hikers and environmentalists have been complaining that streams are drying up and lake levels are being lowered. A little study reveals the problem: the trees are efficiently catching rainfall and holding runoff, and the water isn't getting to streams and ponds. Grass is killed out by the shade, fallen pine needles and lack of water, so wildlife has less forage. Early photographs of the Black Hills show many open meadows among the trees, partly because Indians and buffalo didn't bother to fight forest fires. Now trees choke the hills, and we may actually have done damage to wildlife habitat.

Love of the land is an uplifting sentiment, as well as an often-heard phrase. And it's easy to love places like the Black Hills or the Rocky Mountains. It's harder to develop a passion for less lovely places, like the streets of a city or the barren-looking prairie. But just as loving a person you don't know can be disastrous, so can blind love of the land. Failure to look at the other side of the equation seems to me a common failing; if one baby is wonderful, ten must be better yet. It is hardly profound to say that we must make intelligent, informed choices based on facts rather than naked emotion. Hardly profound, but more important than ever now that we can literally see the end of some of our resources.

A tree is a wonderful thing, especially here where they are rare. The cottonwoods in this pasture pay for their water in shade for the cattle and us, in relaxation for the eye, in shelter for the birds, in a dozen ways. A tree in the right spot is a treasure, but it is possible to have too many trees, or too many in the wrong places.

Once, visiting a friend in Phoenix, Arizona, I shocked passersby and embarrassed my friend by lecturing a man who was spraying water on a vast complex of sidewalks to clean them. It was standard practice, I was told, as they led me gently away. Everyone did it, just as everyone poured gallons of water daily onto vivid green lawns and into swimming pools. Shopping became a study in contrasts between the dry desert heat and the icy inside air. I'd read articles about the water table, and how quickly it would be depleted. "Don't you know the water table will be *gone* by the end of the century?" I shrieked. They knew. But they're proud of having "made the desert bloom," having adapted it to their needs rather than vice versa.

But I'm getting out of my neighborhood. We do the same thing here: underground houses and wood heat would be perfect for our icy winters and blistering hot summers, but costs are high because the houses are different, unusual. Instead we build frame houses, pack the walls with insulation, and listen to our propane heaters roar to keep the place warm in a blizzard.

Refreshed by the drink and by throwing water over each other, we go on down the trail. Twenty two-year-old heifers with their first calves are gathered under a huge tree below the dugout, resting, switching flies, chewing their cuds. The calves aren't quite as big as those of mature cows, but they look healthy, and their mothers are putting on weight. We sit in the truck and watch them a while, remembering for Mike which calves we pulled in the middle of the night in a snowstorm. One morning we found a cow dead, not only her uterus prolapsed but most of her internal organs as well. Beside her nestled a calf. The coyotes had eaten some of the cow's extruded guts, and half the calf's tail. We put him on a cow that had lost her calf, and he is growing up big and tough. He eyes the pickup, his stubby tail twitching, too short to brush flies away.

One heifer sticks her head into the window and licks George's sleeve. He taught her to take cake from his hand last winter, and she hasn't forgotten. Mike puts his hand out, hoping to feel her rough tongue, but his smell is strange to her and she backs off, eyes wide.

Suddenly a calf throws his tail in the air and begins to run toward the dugout. Others follow, then a cow, until the entire bunch is in motion, galloping madly, some of the calves bawling. The heat causes the grubs under their hide to hatch, and the itching makes them run, shaking off the good fat they've spent all summer putting on. They'll run to the dugout, then wade in and cool down.

Seeing the healthy, vigorous calves makes the struggle of calving season, when we checked these heifers every two hours around the clock for two months, seem worthwhile and very long ago.

Tenth Gate:
No Time for Horses

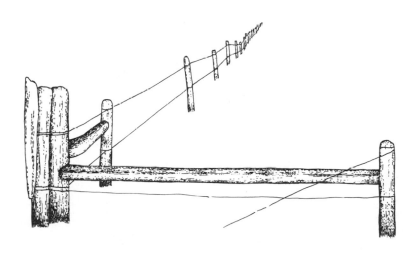

We leave the heifers belly-deep in water and cross another ridge to a set of corrals and a pair of dug-outs—one on our land and one cater-corner from it in the neighbor's pasture we pass through to get to our main summer pasture.

When I first came to the ranch, a well here served both pastures, with a tank divided in half by the fence. But the neighbor and my father had continuous small disagreements, and finally my father contracted with a dragline operator to dig a dugout in our corner. The neighbor happened by before the job was finished and had one dug for himself. Since both dugouts are drawing from the same water source, the water levels stay about even, as long as neither rancher puts in too many cattle.

The next neighbor's pasture is now called the eight-hundred-acre pasture, presumably to distinguish it from the five-thousand-acre pasture. Distinguishing pastures by size rather than by family names indicates one of the changes in ranching in my lifetime: the coming of corporate ranching. A big syndicate can always buy another ranch if one wears out. Sometimes the management of such a ranch isn't as careful about conserving water and grass as a man who owns his land.

For example, we arrived here one blistering July day in a drought year to see at least five hundred thirsty steers milling around the neighboring dugout. The pasture was already overgrazed and couldn't keep that large a bunch content for long. The cattle shoved at the fence, reaching for the grass and clean water on our side. For a month we made daily trips over east to fix the fence and put out the cattle that had gotten in. A herd that size could have finished off in days the grass that kept our cattle fed for that month.

The flexibility of a corporate ranch is enormous. Drought in South Dakota? Move the herd to the ranch's land in Colorado. Prices too high in South Dakota? Buy fence posts by the trainload where they're cheaper, without worrying about the local economy. Cattle prices too low? Sell somewhere else, or write off the loss against company profits, or rent more land and keep the cattle until prices rise. Plow a pasture and plant wheat one year when prices are high, then get a government subsidy to take the ground out of production—extra cash, a bonus, even if you don't get a wheat crop.

The really dangerous part of all this, I think, is that not only is the federal government allowing these damaging habits but it is encouraging and subsidizing erosion—by providing payments for various practices that actually damage soil in the long run. I know teenagers who get $50,000 a year in such payments. Current agricultural wisdom seems to be that one can't make a living by simply conserving, by holding the size of an operation down to what one man or one family can run without costly machinery. The modern idea is growth at any cost. Meanwhile, men who work for a company that is run like a business keep business hours: eight to five, with weekends off. If the fence gets down on a weekend, we fix it and chase out their six hundred head of steers before they eat our entire winter pasture. A great system for them, but not so good for us.

We bounce through the tenth gate, about six miles from home. The pasture beside the trail looks as if it has been plowed, with huge dry clods of earth exposed to the sun. Theoretically, ripping the soil apart as this corporation has done will increase grass production by allowing moisture to penetrate deeper. But it is inappropriate wisdom in this arid region; years will pass before the pasture is smooth enough not to shake a truck to pieces. I hate to ride here to look for our cattle when they get out; the ruts make my horse trip and stagger even at a walk.

Similarly, some corporations in South Dakota are now plowing up huge chunks of virgin native sod to plant grain. Newspaper stories tell of monster tractors that plow over everything, flattening hills, filling in waterways with bulldozers, blasting rock ridges. Neighboring ranches find their dams filling with silt, windblown dust covering fences and drifting everywhere, grass and trees damaged by pesticides used to finish off the native vegetation.

The manager of one of the corporations says a law that would require conservation planning is a law to "prohibit farm expansion." With modern technology, farms of two thousand to five thousand acres can't be profitable; he prefers operations of twenty thousand to thirty thousand acres, with single fields of at least six thousand acres. The underlying assumption seems to be that agriculture of any kind is an industry, to be run like a factory. That assumption does not calculate for animal behavior or the unpredictable in weather or land. With a big enough tractor and enough power you can plow anything, and no end to tractor growth seems to be in sight. The pesticide ads on television show tractors that look two stories high.

I'm also intrigued by the public's inability to distinguish between farming and ranching. Though many ranchers do more and more farming in an effort to diversify their operations and get a profit from something, ranching is still primarily devoted to grazing natural grasses, while farming is a constantly changing effort to plant something new and better. Too many farmers now seem to believe that technology in the form of big tractors, irrigation or pesticides can turn arid grasslands into farming ground. As soon as ranches existed, experts on ranching miraculously appeared. One of them, Walter Baron von Richthofen, never ranched, but that didn't stop him from being an expert. In 1885 he wrote confidently that because of "the high altitude, the dryness of the atmosphere, and the light rainfall . . . cattlemen need have no fear of ever being crowded out by farmers." He was wrong about a few other things, too.

Are the force and crudity represented by huge tractors and killing sprays really required in a world of such precision as ours? For centuries, swallows have flown six thousand miles to arrive at San Juan Capistrano on the same day every year, in spite of weather, war, politics and pollution. No amount of force has changed their habits. Every step we have taken into the

world of technology—even the clearly beneficial ones—
has removed us another step from that kind of instinct,
from that ability to survive, to live in a natural world. We
can't turn off the machines, but we have to start count-
ing the steps, estimating their length, looking at where
we're going.

With interest rates high, the price of ranch land
has tripled in the last thirty years. Perhaps only a
corporation could afford to buy a sizable ranch now.
Since much of our land is already surrounded by corpo-
rate-owned land, we may be especially vulnerable, both
to the damages caused by such management and to the
limitations. The thought of ever selling land we've cared
for to a corporation turns my stomach, but who else
could afford it? Will I have a choice?

If we were to get into debt—borrow money to
buy new machinery, for example—the ranch could
change owners in a hurry. Over the years I've heard so
many versions of one story that I believe it. A rancher
borrowed money for one more year from his local bank.
If he didn't make money that year, he swore to get out.
A spring storm caught all his cows down by the creek and
drove them into the water, where either hypothermia or
freezing killed most of them. The rancher locked the
house, dug the truck out of the snow, drove to town and
threw the keys on the banker's desk. "It's out there, and
it's all yours," he said. The banker looked up and said,
"You got fifty dollars a month until you get back on your
feet. You'd better get some groceries and get out of here
because it's going to snow again." Imagine a banker or

investor doing that today!

A corporation already owns the remains of my grandfather's first homestead. We drive a quarter-mile out of our way to show it to Mike. Not much is left: a few sticks where the house was, a dam he dug by hand. Homesteading in the 1880s was even more precarious than ranching today, so Charles Hasselstrom also worked as a logger and miner in Deadwood, eighty miles away. He left Deadwood Saturday morning, rode to the homestead, spent Sunday there and rode back to Deadwood in time for work on Monday morning.

My uncle Harold has photographs of the horse he rode. "That," he says, "was a horse. They *used* horses in them days. There isn't a horse alive today could do what them horses did all the time, because we don't ride them enough, not like they used to. And they didn't have grain or fancy feed and no veterinarians to take care of them, either."

The whole family sometimes rode horseback over east for church socials. Most of the people in the community would get up early, do chores, ride ten or twenty miles here, eat a lunch brought in by women in the wagons, and perhaps hear a sermon by a traveling minister. They'd spend the afternoon visiting and making ice cream. There would be dancing in the evening, and then the ride home long after dark. They didn't have much money, but they had things they could provide for themselves: food, entertainment, work.

Somehow, as soon as a few improvements came along, the horse became obsolete. According to Wes

Tenth Gate

Jackson, of The Land Institute in Kansas, "The idea that a horse is low technology and a tractor is high ought to be turned around. The horse is many times more technically sophisticated than the machine." I agreed, even before I saw a letter in *Time* magazine from a woman in Connecticut. She wrote, "Surely you jest when you report that the government has spent $5 million to develop the Hexapod, an off-road vehicle that does 8 mph over hilly, rocky or swampy areas and can be guided forward, backward or to the side. Gadzooks, I have had one for years. It is called a horse, and it walks without the aid of 16 onboard computers."

Unfortunately, the government isn't kidding. I think we've reached a state of ridiculousness where it's no longer possible to collect a set of facts and predict a logical outcome.

Horses were cheaper than four-wheel-drive pickups burning foreign oil; they still are, but modern ranchers want to do things faster, cover more ground. We don't have time for horses, and it seems to me we don't have time for ice cream socials, either, or quilting bees or barn raisings. We're constantly searching for speed and efficiency. We even buy appliances that cook faster, ignoring the fact that most "fast food" has no flavor.

I've never tasted Hopi blue corn from plants that are hand tended and given a cupful of precious water at a time. I'm told it's wonderful, but of course it has no place in the modern world. It's not efficient to grow tiny, tasty ears of corn in a desert when we can grow ten thousand acres of soft, mushy corn in flat ground with pesticides and chemical fertilizer. It's not efficient to grow the tomato I'll pick when I get home this afternoon the way I grow it, with hand labor. By modern standards, because I have a college degree, my time is considered too valuable to waste on physical work. By contrast, in Bali, making something beautiful by hand is considered devotion to the gods. As I bite through the taut skin of my home-grown tomato and let the fragrant, tart juice run down my throat, I'll think in scorn of the tomatoes grown efficiently, the pale pink ones in the supermarket that taste like cotton. And thank the gods of gardening.

My auto mechanic tells me it's too expensive to fix the pickup ignition now; they throw away the entire unit and put in a new one. My telephone is designed to quickly connect me with anyone in the world, but today I can't call my neighbor, a mile away, because the telephone's computer is down—my punishment for trying to save time by phoning instead of driving over for coffee and a real visit with her. A manager tells me it's "too much trouble" for a chain supermarket to make the waste from its fruit and vegetable department available for compost and chicken feed. Instead, to prevent indigents from eating the food—"they might get sick and sue the store"—gallons of bleach are poured over it in the dumpster. The bleach doesn't seem to bother my chickens; in fact, the county agent says it may help rid them of internal parasites.

Meanwhile, people in this community whose families made it through the 1930s without any kind of government assistance now take commodity foods. Some need the food, because their income—from ranching or other jobs—isn't enough. Others take it because everyone else does, or in the cynical belief that if they don't, the government will waste it, or because they believe their taxes will pay for storage until the food is gone. Virtually everyone here recently signed up for rice, honey, butter, cheese and milk; some went back three times. Friends in other agricultural communities report families who refuse commodities are eating only bread and milk, because that's all they can afford—and farms are specialized now, efficient. Even farmers no longer grow almost everything they need.

Perhaps efficiency does not preclude doing things well, but it seems to me the trend is there. I think we are concentrating so hard on efficiency that many of us don't notice that our lives are low on quality. And before we do notice that, our flavorless existences will be over.

Ahead of the pickup, a coyote leaps straight up out of the coyote-colored grass and streaks away. Mike yells something about shooting him; George grins and speeds up. The coyote glances over his shoulder, flips his tail to the right and swings that way, adding a bit of speed. George speeds up again. Mike reaches over and honks the horn.

The coyote glances back, trips and rolls over three times, puffing dust. George slams on the brakes. The coyote gives us a look that can only be disgust, shakes the dust out of his fur and trots with dignity down a gully.

With no dignity to worry about, the three of us laugh until we're weak, pointing wordlessly at the dust hanging in the air, mimicking the look on the coyote's face.

Eleventh Gate:
Fighting the Prairie Fire

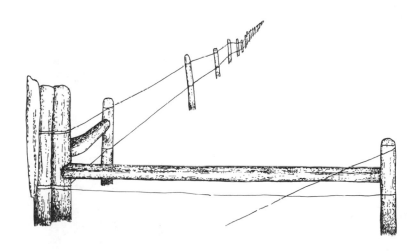

We drive around the end of the neighbor's dugout and through a gate beside our corrals. We tried to corral a bull here last week so we could load him in the trailer and take him home—he'd been visiting the neighbor's cows. Rather than go in the trailer, he tried to jump over the fence; instead, he fell on it and broke the top two planks. We chased him until he was exhausted, roped him, and tried to drag him into the trailer by tying ropes from him to the saddles. He was too heavy, so we drove the pickup up behind him and shoved him inside.

But the corral must be fixed, because we may need it at any time. While George drags new boards out of the pickup and Mike drinks more water, I scan the skyline. I'm looking for anything there is to see: clouds bringing rain or shade, the dust from a pickup or smoke from a prairie fire. Not long ago, on our way home from here with the horses in the trailer, we saw a little thunderstorm form over the Black Hills. As we watched, the cloud blackened, drifted out over the prairie and began shooting shafts of lightning downward. We drove on toward home. The little cloud rolled away. A thin column of smoke began to rise. We speeded up, rushing to get home to join the fire crews.

Today the horizon is clear, but I remember the time it blackened as far as I can see. The fire in March of 1980 was larger than usual, but typical. It began along the tracks, where two neighbors were fixing fence. They'd almost controlled it when a second fire started, and the wind took both out of their hands. By the time I noticed it, the horizon north of the house was a solid wall of fire and smoke. The wind was blowing sixty miles an hour. Just east and a bit north of us smoke from another fire was billowing up.

I yelled "Fire!" along with a few appropriate comments on the railroad, and ran back inside. George and a couple visiting us, Jim and Mavis Potter, were already in motion. I got the pickup and filled a cream can with water while George got gunnysacks from the barn.

The pump trucks, manned by community volunteers, do a lot of the fire fighting, but everyone around who can walk fights fire by hand. We soak gunnysacks in water and beat on the flames wherever we can get close enough. The wet gunnysack gets heavier with each stroke. Whirling it, you strike at the flames once, twice, several times, until they are out in that spot, and then several more times to beat out any sparks and wet down the grass. This effort puts out an area perhaps two feet wide in two or three minutes. You step ahead, gasping with exertion and inhaling smoke, and repeat the operation. Every inch of fire must be beaten out in this way. Cow chips—dried patties of manure—that could smolder for a long time, must be shoveled or kicked into the already burned area.

The four of us worked from the pickup down a little slope and did a respectable job of containing the fire at that point. Then the wind switched, George shouted, and I had to run back and move the pickup because the fire had jumped the line and was racing toward it. We did it all a second time, and then the wind switched to the northeast, so our line was momentarily safe. We stopped for breath until a railroad-yellow truck drove up to us.

The driver said, "Where's the Hasselstrom place? We've got a report that the buildings are about to burn." I looked back toward our house—it was still safe—and asked him to follow us to my uncle Harold Hasselstrom's. When we got there, the fire was still a mile away from the buildings. With about ten people working, we soon had it contained. We gathered at the trucks, panting, covered with soot and wet black streaks where the sacks had soaked us.

Suddenly the wind changed direction, and George and the Potters ran down a little gully where the fire had sent out a new tongue of flame. I pulled the pickup a hundred yards farther from the fire, and another pulled up beside me. The driver and I got out of our trucks and went to the tailgates, reaching for our sacks.

The wind shifted and someone shouted. By the time we leaped into the drivers' seats, the fire was under both trucks. Mine was still running, and I shifted and jammed my foot down on the accelerator, wondering if I was going to be blown up; on TV every little jolt causes a car to explode in flames. The pickups practically collided, but we got to the top of the hill and looked back.

The wind was driving the fire east, away from us but toward Harold's property. A wall of flame west and south hid George and the Potters. Finally we began to see figures moving through the smoke rising from the ground in front of us. We drove cautiously over the smoldering grass, picked up our crews, and searched through the smoke until we found my uncle's buildings.

One man was shouting hysterically, "Get everybody out of that house! It's going to go! Get everybody out!" He ran down the road to his car, and that was the last we saw of him.

George and Jim ran up the hill toward the fire, and someone found a hose and pump and began spraying water on the grass around the buildings. I found Aunt Jo, and suggested she collect a few things in case the house burned.

"Where's Harold?" I was visualizing a struggle to get him—unwillingly perhaps—out of a burning house. He's a big, heavy man who lost one leg to cancer a few years ago, but he goes everywhere on his crutches and no one tells him what to do.

"He's out in the truck somewhere, checking on our calves," she said.

Suddenly I heard a roar, saw a fire truck coming, and ran out in the road to stop it.

"Get to the top of the hill," I told the driver. "It's coming down any second."

"Our orders are to go over south," he said, putting the truck in gear. I screamed imprecations as he drove away.

In a few minutes another fire truck came through, and Jo and I planted ourselves in front of it. The driver turned into the yard, made a pass around the house, spraying water, and turned back, heading south.

I could see George and the Potters running down the hill toward us. Smoke boiled up behind them, and the fire was moving so fast they had to run flat out to stay ahead of it. The wind strengthened. The fire was directly in line with the house.

I stopped another fire truck, and this time all I had to do was point. He roared up the hill and across the fire's front, spraying water. Then he drove away.

The fire and the wind paused. Then a blast of hot air hit us, and the fire jumped the sprayed line and came on. George and the Potters were still running hard. The yard filled with smoke, through which drifted forms carrying sacks, all headed toward the road, their cars and escape.

Jo still refused to leave. "Everything I've worked for is in that house. If it goes, I might as well go with it." She grabbed a shovel and disappeared into the smoke toward the fire.

George stopped running when he found a hose and began spraying a pile of posts behind the machine shed, already smoking. Jim joined him.

Mavis got in the truck with me, and we moved it closer to the road. She was coughing so hard she could barely speak. I left her with the pickup while I went to find my aunt, figuring the three of us might be able to throw her in the pickup too if necessary.

Suddenly the wind shifted yet again. The fire swept down into the dry bed of a dam, exploded a few withered weeds, and died. The smoke cleared.

George and Jim emerged from behind the machine shed; they said later that they had been within seconds of abandoning it, because the metal siding was too hot to touch.

Going Over East

———————————————

East, we could hear motors and shouts as the fire raced down on men fighting there. We jumped into the pickup and went that way, and topped a hill to look down on our ranch. Then we turned back to a small pasture where Harold's fat yearling steers, fed all winter and ready for market, were surrounded by flames and backed against a fence. The steers waited, staring at their hoofs until the flames reached them, then backed up in a bunch and stared until the flames were almost on them again. Their noses were blistered and some of them had patches of burned hair.

We soaked our sacks and beat at the flames until we made an opening so we could drive the steers out. We spent nearly an hour and finally got the flames stopped at the fence line. Then another truck came past, cutting the fence on its way east; the steers slipped past us and followed the truck toward a new fire front. We knew we couldn't drive them back until they quieted down.

Exhausted, we went east to help with the fire at another ranch. On the way we crossed a wide plowed strip where one man had made a fire guard. He had also plowed around some haystacks, not bothering to stop for the two fences in the way. He was laughing and trying to untangle a half-mile of barbed wire and broken posts from the plow.

Nearby, several women sat in trucks, their hair neatly coiffed, their makeup intact. Mavis and I looked at them, and then at each other, and burst into hysterical giggles. Both of us had singed eyebrows, our faces were covered with soot and sweat, and the hair around our faces was burned crisp. Between giggles, we made rude remarks, until George muttered to Jim, "We'd better get them out of here."

It had never occurred to any of us not to help fight that fire, even though not a single spark had fallen on anything we owned. Jim and Mavis live seventy miles away, but they didn't hesitate. Taking responsibility in that manner is one of the old-fashioned qualities of rural life I love; I'm horrified when I hear about bystanders refusing to help stabbing victims in cities.

Since the fire seemed to be under control, we went back to the house. It was nearly 4:00; we'd been fighting fire for almost six hours. After dark we drove down the road to see if anything was still burning. Our way was eerily lit by the red glow of hundreds of burning fence posts, and four of Harold's huge haystacks were still flaming.

I stayed up most of the night watching the sparks from burning railroad ties blow across the tracks into the pasture where our cows were calving. We should have moved them, but didn't think of it until dark, and cows hate to move in the dark. So every hour I'd call the railroad office in Rapid City and ask them to send a truck to hose down their damn railroad ties before they set another fire. I must have started getting on someone's nerves, because about 3:00 A.M. I saw a hose truck moving along the tracks, and sparks disappearing.

Earlier we had discussed the possibility that, if the fire jumped the tracks to our side, where winter grass is high, we would have to fight fire again to save our ranch. "If that fire jumps the tracks," said Jim, a man of few and well-placed words, "we'll have about two minutes to get out of here, and we'll be lucky to make it." I knew he was right. We wouldn't have been able to save anything, even the pets or the cows in the corral.

The fire burned eleven thousand acres of pasture, much of it ungrazed, and extended more than ten miles in length, crossing the creek at one point when burning trees fell across. It might have gone on forever, but ranchers there were waiting for it. At least forty haystacks burned, plus several baby calves and miles of fence; no one estimated the loss in dollars.

None of this, except the size of the fire, is especially unusual. When a fire starts here, this is what everyone goes through. There were probably real heroics that day, judging from some of the stories I've heard—especially about people who were surrounded by fire and saved by others. Ranchers have asked for help from political officials, written letters to the newspapers and to the railroad, but nothing has changed. We have no one to rely on but each other.

Twelfth Gate:
Predators Drive Pickups

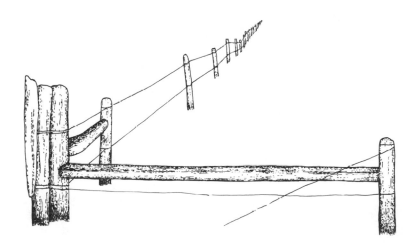

*M*ike opens an easy gate, and we are in our largest pasture over east—about six hundred acres— where the bulk of our cows come in June and remain until the end of July. Then they are moved back to the Lester place and the school section to remain until Christmas, if the grass is good and the winter remains open.

We would keep them here longer, because the pasture could support them, but we lease about half of the pasture from the Bureau of Land Management. Rather than trusting a rancher to assess the grass and remove cattle at the proper time, bureau rules require that we remove the cattle on July 31, no matter how much rainfall we've had or how much grass remains. We can't shut the cattle into the leased land so they can get full use of it, because the leased land has no water.

All over the West ranchers graze cattle on public lands, a matter of serious and growing controversy. Where water is scarce in the desert regions, ranchers with long-term leases have invested money in providing it: drilling wells, providing tanks and dugouts for cattle. Wild animals also use the water, but that doesn't mollify the critics, who charge ranchers with seriously overgrazing the land—and are no doubt right in many cases. Part of the reason for overgrazing may be those large investments in water, together with low cattle prices, but certainly overgrazing should be stopped. However, I question some of the suggested methods. A recent issue of *Earth First!* magazine instructed readers on the quickest method for disconnecting a windmill so water would cease to flow. I can sympathize with the frustration that leads to such direct action—I've taken some pretty direct actions for love of the environment myself—but the author of that article forgot that it is not the rancher who will die of thirst. The rancher may have insurance, and may simply write off the loss, but the cattle—and any wildlife who rely on the water—will suffer the slow agony of dehydration and death.

This type of sloppy thinking angers me most in people who are concerned about the land and its use. Another magazine recently featured a sketch of cows with blood dripping from their jaws, and called them "bovis vampiris profitus." The cattle aren't at fault; they follow their natures, as do all animals. If primitive man had happened to domesticate antelope, or deer, modern critics might be objecting to their grazing habits. If we apply the same logic to our highway death toll, we see that drinking, speed and other human flaws contribute; but instead of modifying behavior, we could end the problem by banning the automobile. We can't take action without thinking of the consequences. Instead of damning cattle, we must work to change government practices that allow abuses of public land. And we must be consistent. If some ranchers are abusing some public land, so are some owners of dune buggies and four-wheelers; no alterations in law should ignore them.

The dam on the land we own, the only source of water in this pasture, is low because of the spring drought, since it's entirely dependent on rainfall and snowmelt. Black mud, heavy with odors, reaches up to the cows' knees before they reach water. We are concerned that calves may be unable to pull themselves out of the mud, or may be tramped down when the cattle crowd in to water. Today most of the eighty calves are drinking near a limestone outcrop that keeps them out of the worst mud. But if the dam gets much lower we can't take the risk; the cattle will have to be moved out before BLM's deadline. Perhaps we can move in some cows without calves, so the grass won't be wasted.

This year BLM has cut the number of cattle that can be grazed on leased land because their employees, sent out to count wildlife, saw fewer deer and antelope. By their logic, our cattle have eaten all the grass, causing the wild ruminants to move away. Actually, last winter was the toughest in a hundred years; snow covered the grass for three months. In one nearby county, ten thousand head of cattle died, and the carcasses of deer and antelope were piled everywhere. Since BLM land is public land, hunters this fall will deplore the poor hunting and cuss the ranchers for ruining their sport.

Five ducks swim in the center of the dam; they have no fear, since we never shoot at them, and even determined hunters seldom get this far. When they do, it usually spells trouble for us. We have no automatic objection to hunters sharing this land with us. But, unfortunately, it seems each time someone does hunt here, we know it because of open gates or cut fence wires, scattered cattle we spend hours on horseback to find, dead ducks floating on the water, deep ruts torn in the muddy spots around the dam, broken fence posts where someone going too fast skidded into the fence.

We'd be delighted to host responsible hunters, but how do we recognize them? It's illegal for us to keep them out of public land, and difficult for us to monitor hunting so far from home. When the grass looks good and game is plentiful, hunters complain about rich ranchers getting pasture cheaply at public expense. But the land looks good because we're careful with it. And hunters' use of the land may do it even more damage for their own purposes—supporting game—than our grazing does. Prairie grass, once it is cured or dried in fall, is brittle and easily broken. A single hunter in a single pickup who insists on driving everywhere he goes can break off and destroy more grass in a day than fifty cows or seventy antelope would eat in a month. When they ask permission, we suggest they park their pickups and walk. For some reason, hunting this way is less attractive, despite the obvious advantages—it's easier to sneak up on game, and a hunter afoot gains in exercise, fresh air and a chance to study the terrain closely.

Most wild animals on our land can live normal lives unbothered by the fact that we live here too. We don't even shoot skunks unless they rip open too many feed sacks and spray inside the barn too often. Since we never shoot at the wildlife we support, none of the animals fear pickups, and even the antelope and coyotes don't always run from us, or the ducks fly. Not much challenge to the hunter who drives around shooting out the window. In addition, we often see other predators here: golden and bald eagles, great horned owls, barn owls, snowy owls migrating south. We tell no one, because it seems that when we do, we find only feathers and bodies on the next trip.

Once my father and I saw a golden eagle strike the ground, then lift with a writhing snake in his claws. He flapped slowly to a fence post and landed, facing us. Father stopped the truck, got out the binoculars, and we looked. I still remember the force of that golden eye as it glared through the black tube of the binoculars into mine. He watched us; we watched him. Finally he bent his glossy neck and tore a piece out of the madly twisting snake, gulped it and looked back at us. Father started the pickup and made a wide circle around him, so he wouldn't fly away. I thought of John McPhee's statement that the first time he saw a red-tailed hawk, he was not sure whether to run or to kneel. By those standards, an eagle merits prostration.

A few days later, Game, Fish and Park officials reported finding the bullet-riddled body of a full-grown golden eagle beside a highway near a town twenty miles north of us.

We drive slowly past the cows to the salt-box. Hot weather seems to increase their consumption, and the bottom of the box is wet and golden, polished smooth as fine silk by rough bovine tongues licking out the last traces of salt. We pour in a bag of loose salt, put the bag back in the truck and weight it with a hammer so it won't blow out. Often we see antelope at salt-boxes, or at spots where we've had them in other years. Sometimes we've startled herds of forty or fifty antelope, a wonderful and hilariously funny sight as they bound away, even though that's more than we care to support. George wonders aloud how long it will be before the population recovers from last winter; we didn't see a single baby antelope this year, and Mike has never seen one.

We drive wide around the dam and lurch through ruts into the BLM section of the pasture. This became public land partly because it proved impossible for homestead-size ranches to be self-supporting in the semi-aridity of the region. Two more homestead remnants hunker down in barren gullies near here, and we can never forget their failure because of the damage they inadvertently caused. Naturally, they plowed part of their homestead land, believing they could create farms here. They were criminally misled; survival on 160 acres of this windswept plateau would have been nearly impossible. I don't know what they planted, but their plowing destroyed the buffalo grass that is the natural cover out here. When they were gone, someone planted crested wheat grass to hold the dry soil, to keep some of it from blowing away.

Crested wheat grass has some advantages as a forage grass, but it matures and dries up quickly, so it is useful to grazing animals only in the spring. Its roots form clumps six to eight inches tall as soil washes or blows away between plants, so the pasture becomes more bumpy and barren every year. Once the buffalo grass was gone, it did not make a rapid comeback. Researchers struggled for years to collect the tiny seeds and propagate it with no success—until they learned to imitate natural conditions. Buffalo and other native grasses like hard ground littered with stones and old growth to slow the wind and hold moisture. Even then, buffalo grass may not visibly grow for a year or two, because instead of producing stems it's producing roots—reaching deep into the soil searching for water, knowing it can't trust Great Plains weather. In this part of our pasture buffalo grass is coming back naturally and slowly—sixty-odd years after the ground was plowed. A few patches the size of a family dinner table have appeared in the crested wheat grass. In another sixty years perhaps the buffalo grass will predominate once more. If no one plows it again, some of the good topsoil might even remain.

The lesson I've learned from bouncing across this patch of land all my life is that some ground simply can't be plowed without damage so severe as to offset any benefits. Yet the corporations are buying up ranches and plowing land just like this to plant grain crops. They can afford the gamble; if the rain doesn't come, they let the land go back to the bank, or sell it and write off a loss. They can afford the gamble, and the loss, but the state and the world can't. No one can write off the loss in topsoil, or in grass that might have nourished ruminants. If the next owner can't restore the grass, the land becomes barren and disappears from production along with thousands of acres covered yearly by concrete highways, shopping centers and subdivisions.

Furthermore, not all land is as well-designed for grazing animals as the unique grasslands in this area. Many enterprises would not flourish here, but the land is perfectly suited for raising meat in a natural way, with a minimum of interference from technology. Even in a dry year when our cattle must strain water through their teeth from muddy dams, calves gain weight and cows are fat because of the nutritive value of the grasses. With lean beef in demand, a state like South Dakota could be in the forefront of a new, safe industry—instead of trying to attract dangerous and damaging ones. In the late 1800s Baron von Richthofen declared, "The climate of the West is the healthiest on the earth; the pure, high mountain air and dry atmosphere are the natural remedies, or rather preventives, against sickness among cattle in general, and against all epidemic diseases in particular; for nowhere in the Western states do we find any traces of pleuro-pneumonia, foot or mouth, and such like contagious diseases. The pure, clear water of the mountain rivers affords to cattle another health preserver, and the fine nutritious and bountiful grasses, and in winter the naturally cured hay, furnish to them the healthiest natural food."

We haven't kept the West quite as pollution-free as the baron saw it, but several western states still boast the purest air and water in the nation. Where nature has seemingly designed a region for the growing of protein on the hoof, why struggle to do something else with it? Why lock cattle in muddy feed lots and pour corn down them for a cholesterol-rich product when, by simply managing grazing lands, we could produce a lean, organic meat acceptable to more people?

Instead, we are treating these grasslands as if we still believed in the Great American Desert, and losing grazing and farmland at an alarming rate. How much can we afford to lose? Even though many people are now avoiding beef, fearing additives or fat, how much beef production ground can we lose before we can no longer feed our growing population?

When explorers first saw the Great Plains, buffalo almost covered the grasslands, wandering at will to find grass and water. No one really knows how many buffalo the prairie supported; estimates varied wildly. But clearly the region was ideal for grazing, and the idea of cattle ranches took root quickly. Before long, the buffalo were nearly extinct and cattle had taken their place to benefit from the rich grass. Baron von Richthofen called the Great American Desert "the largest and richest grass and pasture region of the world, and... it will probably soon become the most important beef-producing country of the globe." He analyzed expenses and profits, and predicted that any properly run ranch could make its owner a true "cattle king," rich beyond imagination. His analysis of the potential for beef production on the plains was correct, but he was no prophet.

We jounce across a cow trail a foot deep, worn by cattle going to water at the dam. Thirty years ago I was walking along this trail, bringing cows out of the BLM land on foot on a day this hot. I don't know why I was walking, but my father has always believed in healthy exercise, especially for the young, so he may have simply talked me out of bringing the horse. I noticed and picked up two curious stones. Each weighed probably five pounds. One, I know now, was a flint core from which arrowheads were struck. The other was a metate, its concave surface worn smooth with grinding.

I could picture the travelers, on a day this hot, dragging themselves across this dusty flat on the way to the blue mountains for the fall hunting. Perhaps the pieces fell from a pack unnoticed; perhaps the people were tired, hungry, starving, and the stones became something to be sacrificed. I believe a woman was carrying them, and a child on her hip, and could no longer carry both.

I picked them up, knew they were old and stood in the hot sun a minute weighing them. Squinting, I tried to estimate how far I would have to carry them before I reached the gate or before my father, leading the cows in the pickup, stopped to pick me up. I put them down on the short grass beside the deep trail, where I was sure I could find them again. Not long after, I read an archaeology article, discovered what they were and went back to look for them. I've been looking for thirty years.

I seem to have an insatiable desire for seeing metaphors in ordinary incidents, and here is another. It is easy to drop something that seems too heavy, but finding it when you need it might be a problem. In our pioneering days—not so long, in the world's terms, after those footsore primitive wanderers—we were pretty casual with our treasures. We chopped down trees, plowed land; we dammed and dug and drilled. We hastily shed our own primitive ways and tried to civilize the natives by cutting their hair, stuffing them into uncomfortable suits. We ignored their religion and scoffed at the idea that they might have a philosophy, let alone one we might use. Now hordes of us are desperately trying to merge with the land, relearn skills and habits long outmoded by modern technology. Is it too late?

I notice a clump of Indian turnip beside the trail, then several more. A few years ago, the plants were so rare here I merely observed them, never dug them up. But today I see two dozen plants in this one location, and I know of several others, so it's time for Mike to have another lesson. All three of us whip out pocketknives and dig separate plants, peel the thumb-size bulb and slice off a white, crunchy round of the tuber. Mike watches skeptically as George and I chew, swallow and slice off another piece. Simultaneously, both of us clutch our stomachs and fall to the ground, writhing and moaning. Mike shrugs, bites into his, and, while we dust each other off, nibbles another tiny bite of the still-grubby root he has peeled. He's surprised by the flavor, which somewhat resembles a potato. When he has finished, he starts peeling another root, half-listening to my speech about Indian women digging them with pointed sticks, braiding the stems and hanging them in the lodge to dry for winter use. Not long ago, we parked beside a car that had four huge braids of dried turnips—several hundred—hanging from the rearview mirror. By the Custer Had It Coming bumper sticker, we knew this was an Indian family who follows some of the old ways.

Often on our drives over east, I carry books that identify flowers and grasses of this region to expand my knowledge. We try to remember places where edible plants grow. We've threatened to give Mike a survival test when he's older, by dropping him off in this pasture with nothing but a knife to see if he can stay a day or two. We ought to try it ourselves, but we say we're too busy.

The Plains Indian tribes collected a surprising variety of plants that are still available where the land hasn't been plowed. Besides the familiar berries—buffaloberries, gooseberries, chokecherries, plum, sand cherries, grapes—we could, at the right time of year, eat salsify roots, raw or cooked Indian turnips, biscuit root, dandelion greens and roots, horsemint seeds (washed down with horsemint tea), mariposa or sego lily roots, the boiled or baked seeds and greens of vetch, and milkweed flowers, buds and greens. We could eat yucca blooms and sagebrush seeds, use yucca roots for soap, and make hair tonic from sagebrush. With a little study, we could do much more.

Whenever I get started on a discussion of wild edible plants, another of my favorites, I wonder how many vital nutrients primitive peoples got in wild foods that we have removed from our packaged, processed, sterile, chemical-laden products. Probably if one knew how to analyze the facts, one could find the reason primitive peoples were healthy running around barefoot wearing only a loincloth, while we eat more, wear more clothes and are increasingly susceptible to disease, tooth decay and degeneration.

Naturally, most of us are not willing to spend all our time gathering our daily roots from the pasture, but I wonder what we have lost. When I hear about the losses to science from the destruction of jungles, I wonder how many plants we have lost in the less exotic surroundings of the prairie that might have benefited us in ways we will never discover. Along with the decline in our physical strength has apparently come a determination that even—or perhaps especially—the weakest of us must survive. The primitive woman who dropped the metate would be puzzled to see her descendants hooked to machines that breathe for us.

To the north of us a few miles, part of the ditch for the water project that injured our calves has been stopped by a young woman archaeologist who has discovered several important prehistoric Indian sites. The pieces I found that day might have given her information I could not read in them. The civilization of those early people left so few traces on the land, we know almost nothing about them—unlike our own, which heaps garbage so high it can be seen from outer space.

I have never minded the evidences of prior habitation here. I don't even mind the unsightly remains of old cars, bedsprings, holed kettles and broken bottles that mark where the homesteaders lived. But modern detritus—cigarette butts, beer cans, McDonald's wrappers (eighty miles across country from the nearest golden arch), even shotgun shells—disturbs me. The old homesteaders lived here, after all, and buried their garbage as neatly as they could in the hard ground. If they left their rusting car bodies behind, it was because they took the motor with them in a newer car, or sold it for a railroad ticket.

The modern junk is left by people who drive in here to indulge in a little recreational killing, or who throw garbage or a cigarette out a car window without thinking of the consequences. For these people, the land is here to provide them with a few hours' sport, a day's relaxation away from the office, or meat they don't need for survival. They see the land as empty, unused, and thus a fit place for garbage or fun. A forest service motto is "Land of Many Uses." I have always believed that for many people the word *use* implies to "use up" or, as the dictionary has it, "to expend or consume, to use up the entire allowance."

For me, this land is as cherished as a tiny backyard, a place my father and people before him have devoted their lives to keeping green, growing, productive, clean and open. They make use of the land in such a way that it retains much of its value. Yet simply because the public cannot easily visit here, it is assumed that we greedy land barons are hoarding it, keeping and abusing it for ourselves. We forget that if the public is allowed into a fragile area, they can destroy it with their love. Yet examples of such damage are numerous in our national parks, and sooner or later we'll have to solve the problem of too little park and too many people.

Once, walking beside a river in Glacier National Park, I found a filled garbage bag tucked behind a tree, where the next high water would rip it loose and scatter the contents. Filled with righteous zeal, I opened and explored it, and found a letter to a traveling son with his parents' return address. I mailed the bag to them, with an anonymous note expressing my belief that they didn't teach him to litter. Because I didn't quite have the courage to sign my name, I have always wondered about their reaction. If I could discover who leaves garbage in our pasture and along our driveway, I would deliver it to the front lawn of their home in town. Or so I have often threatened. They would be shocked, outraged; I would probably be arrested. But their yard and mine are the same: part of our homes. It should not matter that mine is larger.

I do not see this attitude as arrogance. We know we cannot own this land, though some faded paper in a dingy office says we do. We are taking care of it for the future. I hope the future doesn't decree that our cattle will be replaced by trailer parks set in tiny lots. But if that is the way the national urge for reproduction decrees, the new residents will find our land as green, as filled with wildlife, as well-watered as we can manage—if the industries don't suck the water away first. It will be pure and beautiful, undamaged and in most cases improved by those of us who have lived on it.

We jounce over the crested wheat grass, sweating and silent, each of us glancing out over the Badlands to the east. The land seems to ripple with heat waves. If I half-close my eyes, I can't see the fences or the distant electric towers; the land beyond the puny strip plowed by the homesteaders disappears into the distance. I can see the earth stretch, flex its muscles. Fence wires tighten, hum, snap and disappear. The earth lies under the sun as it did ten thousand years ago—clean, ready for the buffalo's track and the human footprint.

Once when Mike was about six years old, we backpacked high into the Big Horn Mountains of Wyoming. We camped above timberline, and while George stalked the wily trout, Mike and I played hide-and-seek with pikas among the tumbled boulders. I had a tendency to be pedantic even with a six-year-old, and we spent part of the day filling our packs with rusty beer cans and other detritus. Resting, we sat on a boulder and stared at the snowy peaks, glowing with sun. Mike sighed. "I could just die for this land," he said. I don't remind him of it now, but I stare at him a moment. His face is maturing; I wonder if he remembers. I'd like to tell him that a lot of people would die for the mountains; what we need are people willing to die—or at least fight—for the prairies.

On top of a low ridge are the scattered bones of a cow. A year ago we were collecting cattle from the pasture on a hot day. I didn't ride to the south end, because all the cattle were sure to be at the dam during the hottest part of the afternoon. As we topped a rise going north with the cows I glanced back instinctively—and saw a cow that seemed to be lying on a hilltop.

I rode to the pickup, where my father looked at her through the binoculars.It was definitely a cow, but she seemed to be lying down. He said we weren't going back after her until we'd separated the cattle we'd come for; it was too hot. "Maybe she'll catch up to us."

We went on and collected the cattle to put in the Lester pasture. When the day was finished we were too tired and hot to go back. Next time we went over east I saw the cow in the same spot. We drove down. She had exploded with heat. We didn't want to get close enough to see if she'd been shot or hit by lightning. We could still recognize her, one of our best young cows; her death cost us thousands of dollars in calves she might have raised.

"Well," my father said, shrugging, "no wonder she didn't catch up with us."

Returning:
Profit, Loss and the
Taste of Vinegar

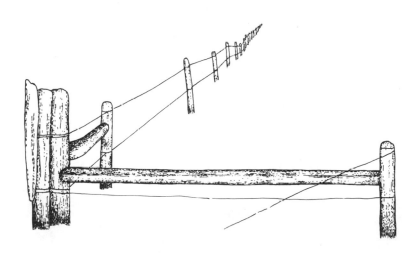

*D*riving slowly over the bumps, we reach the south end of the pasture and the reason we came over east today. The ditch that has illegally crossed our land is empty; no calves in it. We will make this long drive daily, to check it until it's filled with dirt. The calf at home will probably die. It wasn't an intentional trespass; the diggers just got lost. Easy to understand, where there are few obvious landmarks. The Water Users' Association needs the water, and the loss of one or two calves isn't worth disrupting old family and community friendships. We know how important water is in a year like this; a cow can drink fifty gallons a day.

We stand by the truck, stretching, and get out our water jug. It almost burns our mouths and tastes of the vinegar the jug originally held. Mike spits out the first mouthful. I splash some on his shirt; it evaporates in a minute, and he's surprised as the hot wind makes him feel cool. I soak my handkerchief and bathe my face; the handkerchief comes away caked with dust. I rinse it again, rub it over the back of my neck, squeeze water down the front of my shirt. Both of us chase George around the truck twice, trying to dump water on him. But he's too agile and we're too hot to chase him far.

I think of Phoenix and the air conditioning, but how can you appreciate being cool if you've never been this hot? In two hours or so, we'll be home, but our house won't be much cooler than outdoors. We could retreat to the basement if we're really miserable, but probably we'll take ice cubes and glasses to the shade of the front porch, where I put a gallon jug of water containing four tea bags this morning. All day the sun has focused on that jar, and by now the tea is strong and brown and warm. We'll pour it, watch the ice melt, hold the sweating glasses against our foreheads. Mike will try to put an ice cube down George's shirt, and the dog will beg one to crunch at our feet. Gradually, as nature intended, we'll cool off, and our bodies and minds will hold a deep appreciation for the sweat-damp shirt and the cool breeze, a gratitude heightened by how hot we've been. Later we'll take turns in the shower, eat sandwiches and a huge salad—lettuce, cucumbers, radishes, nasturtium blossoms, green onions, spinach collected from our garden—and return to the porch to wait for the evening wind and watch the sun go down.

Three stomachs growl in unison. The sun beats on our heads. East, heat waves ripple over the Badlands Wall, which seems a mile away instead of fifty. Mike stares wistfully and reminds us he's never been to the Badlands. He'd be happy to go right now, driving across country to the east, where little gullies begin practicing to turn into rugged arroyos. We talk him out of the notion, but make rash promises.

The last time I looked for cattle there with my father, he told me a story as we rode. Homesteaders tried to make farms even out of the forbidding alkali flat that flickers with mirages today. On one occasion a homesteader's wife had gone to town for supplies. A distant neighbor couldn't reach the man by telephone after several days, and went looking. The homesteader's horse stood in the yard, saddled. The house was empty.

Returning

After several hours the searchers were tired, puzzled—and thirsty. One dropped a bucket down the well for a drink. Instead of splashing, it thumped.

Once a brave man had been lowered into the well and drawn the body up, a coroner said he thought the man had been killed by falling into the well headfirst. He'd been there, in the official opinion, about the same length of time the man's wife had been visiting in town. The man was buried, and his widow sold the barren homestead and found a job in town that allowed her to raise her children in comfort.

Now, looking out over the pasture where the man homesteaded, at the alkali flats glittering in the sun, we see familiar shapes: buffalo (technically *Bison bison*) back on the lands where we still drive through their water-filled wallows every spring. Our big neighboring ranch is experimenting with six hundred cows, testing the market for leaner meat with a product that is naturally adapted to this grasslands paradise. It's a great idea; we'd like to consider it ourselves, but it will create a new set of problems. A fence that will hold a cow won't necessarily hold a buffalo; when buffalo are ready to move, they go wherever they want, and normal fences barely slow them down.

We're all reluctant to head for home. I'm staring around at the fence that needs fixing; at the back of my mind I wonder what I was thinking, to have come back here when I could be teaching comfortably in a college. I love the country, but I feel guilty when, as now, George and Mike seem to see nothing in it but hard work for small rewards. For me, the sight of an eagle floating over a pasture is reward enough for a week. But rewards like that don't buy new machinery.

Groaning, we get back in the truck, into the seat that seems to set our thighs on fire. We are, by the odometer, eleven miles from the house. The plains fry in the sun; the Black Hills to the west look cool and distant. George turns north, following a cattle trail.

The day's work isn't over. We return to the dam and drive slowly through the cows resting there. We're looking for tight bags: cows with so much milk in their udders it would indicate their calves have not sucked today. If we see such a cow, we might be able to identify the mother of the injured calf at home, perhaps in time to get the cow back and give the calf a better chance of survival. Or we might discover that another calf is lost or sick.

We also count bulls. In this season most ranchers have their bulls with their cows, and bulls in adjoining pastures often fight, break down the fences, mix the cattle. We've brought horses here several times this summer to move our neighbors' big Longhorn bulls out of the pasture; we already know we'll have some crossbred Longhorn calves. This creates additional problems in birth, since the Longhorns' huge horn structure may be too large to permit some of our cows to bear such a calf without a Caesarean. Later, when we sell our calves, the odd-colored ones will be separated by sale officials and bring less money. We can only hope that the bunch of buffalo that passed through a few weeks ago didn't leave any crossbred offspring behind.

As we look at the calves we check for swelling between the hindquarters caused by last month's castration, and for open wounds over the brands. The heat and flies increase the danger of such wounds, and a calf could be dead in a day or two from an untreated sore. The calves look good, grass fat, leaping around us with that excess of energy that shows they're doing well.

Mike asks how much money we'll make when the calves are sold, and I realize he's never seen us sell cattle; he's always gone by that time. I explain the process to him, and he's astonished to discover that the rancher doesn't know until the sale is over if his year's work will be profitable or not. Trucking the cattle to the sale ring costs several dollars a calf, not to mention costs assessed at the sale ring for feed, brand inspection and a beef promotion tax. If our expenses are too high, we may actually sell our year's work at a loss.

All summer checking the cattle, the spring work of calving, the winter's feeding—all that is movement toward the day this fall when we'll sell the calves and learn whether our year's work has made a profit or not. The tension of waiting shimmers in the air like the heat waves over the Badlands. We'll feed the smaller, thinner calves until spring and sell them sometime next year, after another six months of work and expense. As compensation, spring prices may be higher. And they may not.

Once we've determined that no bulls are missing, and the cows seem quiet, we get a rough count and head for home. We have no watch, but our stomachs and the sun's position tell us it's almost two in the afternoon. We go back to the Lester pasture and its seven precious trees; there aren't any in the leased pasture. The cattle stand in the shade of most of the big cottonwoods, but we find a small one with only two cows under it. The air is alive with flies and the smell of fresh manure, but we're used to that. With the pickup doors open, we may catch a little breeze.

Mike soaks his shirt again, sloshes water on me, and sprints after George, who dashes away with surprising speed for a big man on a hot day. They disappear behind a tree, Mike calling to me, "Don't look!" I find privacy behind another tree. When they get back I slap canned meat and spread on bread and hand out little containers of yogurt or canned fruit, refreshing in the heat, for dessert.

It's during these times that I've heard many of the stories about this country that feed my imagination. A sandwich in one hand, coffee cup steaming on the dashboard, my father would be silent awhile, and then get started. "I remember one time when Frank told me about wintering over here someplace in a cabin with two other guys. They'd been out all day, feeding cows or something, and had come in for supper. They had quite a lot to drink, and got good and drunk, and kind of staggered off to bed. The third guy, I don't remember his name, he'd been sick, and along in the middle of the night Frank woke up and got up to put more wood on the fire. The other guy had fallen out of his bunk and was lying on the floor. Frank went over to wake him up, and he grabbed his shoulder to shake him, and he was stiff.

"So Frank woke up the other guy—I can't tell you his name, I think he's still alive—and they looked the third guy over and he was deader than a doornail and frozen solid. Maybe the drink. Anyway, the other guy started to laugh, a real high, shrill laugh, and he laughed and laughed and laughed. Frank said he stood it for about two hours and then he saddled up and got out of there; he said you never heard anything like that laugh. He couldn't take it."

The harshness of the prairie takes people strangely. Many, like the laughing man, have broken under the pressure. A windstorm here almost always lasts three days without letup. When wind has been howling in the window frames for three days, I can understand the pioneer women who went insane in their dusty sod shanties, without a tree or stalk of green in sight. I wonder if I am one of them, or will be when I am old—if I am still on this land. I wonder if I will have to choose between this land and a husband who is talking of getting a job in town, getting away from the endless isolation of winter, the silence, the wind, the cattle. I wonder if our son's cowboy dreams will evaporate as he learns the cost of TV sets, VCRs, cars, food.

What is it that I will inherit?

We eat, sit in the shade, talk. George and I drink hot coffee from a thermos; Mike, our personal representative of the next generation, drinks a can of pop we put next to a piece of ice in the cooler. But it's not as chilled as it would be from the pop machines he's used to, and he sips at it with disdain. He can't understand why we don't have a better cooler; he's not sure why we came over here. All we did was drive past the cattle. Why couldn't we have gone swimming?

Wearily, we pack up the trash from lunch and climb into the pickup. Before we've driven far, I can smell smoke. I look around, but we're in the Lester hollow and can't see the distant horizons. George smells it too, and we drive to the top of a rocky hill to get a better look. Nothing. But the smell is strong now, close. Mike opens the truck door and gets out for a drink of water. The smell is suddenly overpowering.

Cursing, I scramble out of the truck, drop to my knees and look underneath, where the catalytic converter hangs low enough to brush the grass. It's not that, but weed seeds have been caught in an angle of the drive shaft, and are blazing furiously—inches from the gas tank. I grab the water jug, tell Mike to get away from the truck, crawl underneath and begin trying to throw water up onto the hot fire. On the other side, George has dumped part of another water jug on a sack and is lying on his back trying to beat the flames out. For one instant we look into each other's eyes and wonder what we're doing here. Mike screams. In another moment the fire is out. George drives ahead, and Mike and I stamp out sparks while George inspects the drive shaft. We lean against the truck, gasping.

We stop at the Lester spring to fill the water jug. Mike looks at the moss and frogs floating in the water and wonders if he could safely drink from the tank.

"Sure," I say cheerily. "Cow slobber isn't any dirtier than your saliva. Might even be cleaner, since they don't eat meat."

He swallows and reaches for the dipper with an air of martyrdom.

I watch him drink water from the pocket in the earth that Silas tapped sixty years ago; the water level must be about the same—a rare thing in the West. Drops cascade off Mike's chin, eroding channels in the dust. I wonder about the ranch he says he'd like to inherit. It's easy to list the negatives: corporate ranching damages the land and economy, as does overuse of chemicals; too much borrowing can overbalance a ranch; big machinery has changed ranching life, perhaps too much.

When the buffalo first grazed this country, it was unfenced; they moved with the seasons, getting maximum use from the grasses without overgrazing in most areas. We changed the rules by fencing off pieces of land, so we can no longer return to completely natural methods of grazing. But within that limitation, we could still go a long way toward allowing the cow to reach its potential as a ruminant by returning to some of the original cattlemen's methods. The cell theory—holistic management—is a partial attempt to utilize the grasses in such a way as to encourage the hardier native species while getting rid of weeds and pest grasses without herbicides. Until the early 1900s, for example, most ranchers made no attempt to feed their herds through the winter. The cattle remained in pastures and ate available grass while the ranchers cared for the other livestock carried on their more diversified spreads. In spring they would find the carcasses of weaker, older animals—but they calculated for the loss.

Now we feed cattle special mixtures to aid growth, prevent infections and disease; we call the vet if a steer sneezes or a cow complains of a headache. Some disease prevention is necessary—epidemic diseases could devastate the industry. But why not move toward a more natural cycle in other areas of care? We have turned a useful job—that of veterinarian—into an industry that may ultimately work against us by helping us create a cow that has no natural immunity, but relies on artificial medication to survive. Meanwhile, some older breeds of cattle have disappeared, as market demand has changed from short, fat cattle to tall, lean, bony ones. Reducing bloodlines to only a few, and making those dependent on medication rather than hardiness to survive, is a recipe for disaster; a new disease, resistant to proven methods, could decimate cattle herds.

If cattle grazed in winter, we would have to preserve pasture for them, reducing overgrazing. Some ranchers allow grass to be grazed to the roots, knowing they will feed all winter and assuming the grass will recover in spring. If cattle grazed in winter, we could do without the monster tractors to feed hay, contraptions to roll it into ever-larger bales, larger trucks to haul it, cash to buy supplementary feed and vitamins. When the herd had been winnowed down to its stronger members, we would spend less money on medicine and vet bills, and would have a more truly organic, leaner product. In years with a bad winter kill, the price of beef would rise with demand; in other years it might be lower. Instead of studying agribusiness and computers, young ranchers might study their areas' biological cycles, learn about grasses and raising work horses to replace tractors, about weed control that doesn't involve poisons. More young farmers would gain their dream: a farm of their own, because with horses we would all have to manage smaller acreages.

We have tried to change nature to fit not only our needs and desires but our whims. We should seriously consider a period of adapting ourselves to nature's laws, before our damage is irreversible.

We have a friend named Zeke who looks at the world a bit differently than most people do. The first time I saw him, at a gathering of folks who love black powder guns and the fur trapping era they belonged to, he was cleaning his tin dinner plate by wiping it on his breechclout. When I objected to the unsanitary nature of this practice, he showed me his alternate method, which his children were using: to scoop up dirt and gravel in the plate and shake it to scour particles of food away, and *then* wipe it on a dress or breechclout. This way he saved water, which was often scarce in the mountain camps, and didn't have to bother with dish soap, towels and other gear he considered nonessential. His children were never sick.

For a time, Zeke lived alone in a house that was overrun with mice. He didn't mind sharing the house, so long as the mice weren't in bed with him or eating his food. He considered the problem, then obtained two plain pine coffins from a local dump. He slept in one and put his food in the other. "It's dandy," he explained. "When I get up in the morning I just shut the lid. If they get friendly during the night, I sleep with the lid shut, too."

Zeke adapted to his environment, rather than forcing his environment to fit him. Most of us might consider that he carried adaptation a bit far, but he's still pursuing his ways, and his children are great people.

I have a list of solutions for the problems ranchers face, but most of them are sheer fantasy: encouraging cooperation between ranchers, as the Amish do, sharing machinery and labor. I have a dream of how this ranch could be run if one person could devote full-time labor to the garden, another to repairs and fencing, another to cattle management, another to preparing well-balanced meals and cleaning the house. Of course, I would be available for advice, but I would be writing most of every day. We would be more nearly self-sufficient, and need less cash. Unfortunately, the family isn't large enough, or young enough, and the idea of communal living sends South Dakota ranchers to the closet to check their rifles. Getting ranchers and farmers—an obstinate lot—to cooperate has always been a problem in changing the agricultural system. Back in the days when the National Farmers' Organization was trying to promote the holding of farm products until the price went up, and dramatizing their cause by dumping milk, many ranchers growled, "Nobody's gonna tell me what to do," and sold anyway.

Or we could preach the gospel of bioregionalism, until each region becomes as nearly self-sufficient as possible. Perhaps we should rise up and do serious battle with the attitude that progress only involves getting bigger, buying more, being further in debt. Movements toward leaner and more organic beef give me hope for a change in the public appetite that would allow us to remain here. Some of these ideas might actually work, but probably only after some great upheaval that throws a lot of ranchers and farmers off their land, and makes people desperate for the red meat they now scorn.

What will I inherit? Perhaps nothing that I don't already have: the knowledge and love of the land I have gained from my father and from my own absorption in this unique world.

When I went to graduate school, professors, who were mostly male, urged me to abandon my provincial attitudes and think about larger issues—things like Truth, Beauty and sonnets. I hunched over my books, trying desperately to understand something called transformational grammar; I studiously tried to understand Sartre. My professors smiled indulgently at my rural ideas, and joked that I actually believed South Dakota was the center of the universe. I value the education I received there; I still re-read the American literature that I studied and later taught. But when I came home on vacation, I began to notice the difference between the old, white-haired, shuffling professors of sixty-five who were due to retire soon, and the vigorous, sun-browned, straight-backed ranchmen of eighty-five around me, still fighting with their sons and insisting "the boy" couldn't handle things if they retired. I wasn't sure then what I was seeing; after all, those old professors were urging me to give up the brutal life of physical labor to which the ranch would tie me, and enter the exciting world of the mind. I now know those professors wasted a lot of my time.

The center of the universe *is* South Dakota. And everywhere else real people are rolling up their sleeves and working toward practical solutions to the problems of supplying water, clean air and food to the multitudes. Many government and industry leaders who should provide us with sound leadership are floundering, caught in a morass of greed, ignorantly applied high technology and hunger for power.

Sometimes, watching a hunting hawk cruise air currents, I experience a moment when it seems all my questions are answered, a moment of clear vision that stuns me with its simplicity and promise. Then it is gone, and I am uncertain again—but the memory sustains me: a solution is possible. The answer might not save this ranch or me—but it can be found.

The trip home from over east always seems to go more quickly, in spite of the many gates between us and a cold drink, and shade. We squint into the glare of the sun as though trying to see beyond the horizon.

Suggested Reading

Hundreds of books giving general information about ranching in the grasslands of the West exist; this list includes those I find especially enjoyable.

Adams, Alexander B. *Sunlight and Storm: The Great American Plains.* New York: G. P. Putnam's Sons, 1977.

Allen, Durward L. *The Life of Prairies and Plains.* New York: McGraw-Hill, 1967.

Berry, Wendell. *A Continuous Harmony: Essays Cultural and Agricultural.* New York: Harcourt Brace Jovanovich, 1970.

_____. *Farming: A Hand Book.* New York: Harcourt Brace Jovanovich, 1967.

_____. *The Gift of Good Land: Further Essays Cultural and Agricultural.* San Francisco: North Point Press, 1981.

_____. *The Long-Legged House.* New York: Ballantine, 1971.

Bourne, Eulalia. *Woman in Levi's.* Tucson: University of Arizona Press, 1967.

Cather, Willa. *My Antonia!.* Boston: Houghton Mifflin Co., 1918.

Cleaveland, Agnes Morley. *No Life for a Lady.* Boston: Houghton Mifflin, 1941.

Cuelho, Art, editor. *Breadbasket with the Blues.* The American Farmer Series, Vol. 2. Big Timber, Mont.: Seven Buffaloes Press, 1986.

_____. *From Seedbed to Harvest.* The American Farmer Series, Vol.1. Big Timber, Mont.: Seven Buffaloes Press, 1985.

Dale, Edward Everett. *Cow Country.* Norman, Okla.: University of Oklahoma Press, 1942, 1965.

Dick, Everett. *The Sod-House Frontier: 1854-1890.* New York: Appleton-Century, 1937.

Ehrlich, Gretel. *The Solace of Open Spaces.* New York: Viking, 1985.

Ensminger, M.E. *The Stockman's Handbook.* Danville, Ill.: The Interstate, 1970.

Evans, David A. *What the Tallgrass Says.* Sioux Falls, S.D.: Center for Western Studies, 1982.

Fite, Gilbert D. *The Farmers' Frontier: 1865-1900.* New York: Holt, Rinehart & Winston, 1966.

Gilfillan, Archer B. *Sheep: Life on the South Dakota Range.* Minneapolis: University of Minnesota Press, 1928.

Green, Ben K. *Wild Cow Tales.* New York: Ballantine, 1969.

James, Will. *Cow Country.* Lincoln: University of Nebraska Press, 1973.

Jeffers, Jo. *Ranch Wife.* Garden City, N.J.: Doubleday and Co., 1964.

Jennings, Dana Close. *Cattle on a Thousand Hills.* Aberdeen, S.D.: North Plains Press, 1968.

Johnson, Jerry Mack. *Country Wisdom.* New York: Anchor, 1974.

Jones, Bryan. *The Farming Game.* Lincoln: University of Nebraska Press, 1982.

Jordan, Teresa. *Cowgirls: Women of the American West, An Oral History.* Garden City, N.J.: Doubleday, 1984.

Karolevitz, Robert F. *Challenge: The South Dakota Story.* Sioux Falls, S.D.: Brevet, 1975.

Kirk, Donald R. *Wild Edible Plants of Western North America.* Happy Camp, Calif.: Naturegraph, 1975.

Kumin, Maxine. *To Make a Prairie: Essays on Poets, Poetry and Country Living.* Ann Arbor: University of Michigan Press, 1979.

Lea, Tom. *The Wonderful Country.* Boston: Little, Brown and Co., 1952.

Suggested Reading

Lemmon, Ed. *Boss Cowman: The Recollections of Ed Lemmon, 1857-1946.* Lincoln: University of Nebraska Press, 1969.

Macfadyen, J. Tevere. *Gaining Ground: The Renewal of America's Small Farms.* New York: Ballantine, 1984.

McDowell, Bart. *The American Cowboy in Life and Legend.* National Geographic Society, 1972.

McEwen, Inez Puckett. *So This Is Ranching!.* Caldwell, Idaho: Caxton, 1948.

Milton, John R. *The Literature of South Dakota..* Vermillion, S.D.:Dakota Press, 1976.

_____*South Dakota: A Bicentennial History.* New York: Norton, 1977.

Morris, Wright. *The Home Place.* Lincoln: University of Nebraska Press, 1968.

Peterson, Gwen. *The Greenhorn's Guide to the Woolly West.* Aberdeen, S.D.: North Plains Press, 1983.

_____. *The Ranch Woman's Manual.* Aberdeen, S.D.: North Plains Press, 1976.

Quammen, David. *Natural Acts: A Sidelong View of Science and Nature.* New York: Shocken Books, 1985.

Richter, Conrad. *The Sea of Grass.* Cleveland: World Publishing, 1946.

Sandoz, Mari. *The Cattlemen.* New York: Hastings House, 1958.

_____. *Love Song to the Plains.* Lincoln: University of Nebraska Press, 1961.

Schatz, August H. *Longhorns Bring Culture.* Boston: Christopher Publishing Co., 1961.

Snyder, Gerald S. *In the Footsteps of Lewis and Clark.* Washington, D.C.: National Geographic Society, 1970.

Steiner, Stan. *The Ranchers: A Book of Generations.* New York: Alfred A. Knopf, 1980.

Stewart, Elinor Pruitt. *Letters of a Woman Homesteader.* Boston: Houghton Mifflin Co., 1982.

Stockton, Bill. *Today I Baled Some Hay to Feed the Sheep the Coyotes Eat.* Billings, Mont.: Falcon Press, 1983.

Surface, Bill. *Roundup at the Double Diamond: The American Cowboy Today.* Boston: Houghton Mifflin Co., 1974

Van Bruggen, Theodore. *Wildflowers, Grasses & Other Plants of the Northern Plains and Black Hills.* Rapid City, S.D.: Fenske, 1983.

von Richthofen, Walter Baron. *Cattle-Raising on the Plains of North America.* Norman: University of Oklahoma Press, 1964.

Webb, Walter Prescott. *The Great Plains.* Boston: Ginn & Co., 1931.

Wilson, Jim and Alice. *Grass Land,* from series *The Territory of Man.* Polk, Neb.: Wide Skies Press, 1967.

Periodicals

Bloomsbury Review, P.O. Box 8929, Denver, Colo. 80201.

High Country News, Box 1090, Paonia, Colo. 81428.

Northern Lights, P.O. Box 8084, Missoula, Mont. 59807.